Applying Functions to Everyday Life

Erik Richardson

Cavendish
Square

New York

Published in 2017 by Cavendish Square Publishing, LLC
243 5th Avenue, Suite 136, New York, NY 10016

Copyright © 2017 by Cavendish Square Publishing, LLC

First Edition

No part of this publication may be reproduced, stored in a retrieval system, or transmitted in any form or by any means—electronic, mechanical, photocopying, recording, or otherwise—without the prior permission of the copyright owner. Request for permission should be addressed to Permissions, Cavendish Square Publishing, 243 5th Avenue, Suite 136, New York, NY 10016. Tel (877) 980-4450; fax (877) 980-4454.
Website: cavendishsq.com

This publication represents the opinions and views of the author based on his or her personal experience, knowledge, and research. The information in this book serves as a general guide only. The author and publisher have used their best efforts in preparing this book and disclaim liability rising directly or indirectly from the use and application of this book.

CPSIA Compliance Information: Batch #CS16CSQ

All websites were available and accurate when this book was sent to press.

Library of Congress Cataloging-in-Publication Data

Names: Richardson, Erik.
Title: Applying functions to everyday life / Erik Richardson.
Description: New York : Cavendish Square Publishing, [2017] |
Series: Applied mathematics | Includes bibliographical references and index.
Identifiers: LCCN 2016003471 (print) | LCCN 2016013576 (ebook) |
ISBN 9781502619679 (library bound) | ISBN 9781502619686 (ebook)
Subjects: LCSH: Functions--Juvenile literature. |
Mathematical analysis--Juvenile literature. | Mathematics--Juvenile literature.
Classification: LCC QA331.3 .R53 2017 (print) | LCC QA331.3 (ebook) |
DDC 511.3/26--dc23
LC record available at http://lccn.loc.gov/2016003471

Editorial Director: David McNamara
Editor: B.J. Best
Copy Editor: Nathan Heidelberger
Art Director: Jeffrey Talbot
Senior Designer: Amy Greenan
Production Assistant: Karol Szymczuk
Photo Researcher: J8 Media

The photographs in this book are used by permission and through the courtesy of: Brent Lewis/ The Denver Post via Getty Images, cover; Ira Heuvelman-Dobrolyubova/Getty Images, 4; Ann Ronan Pictures/Print Collector/Getty Images, 10; Haihong Zhao/Shutterstock.com, 15; jorisvo/ Shutterstock.com, 17; michaeljung/Shutterstock.com, 22; sumroeng chinnapan/Shutterstock.com, 30; kropic1/Shutterstock.com, 33; granata68/Shutterstock.com, 41; Alenavlad/Shutterstock.com, 44; isak55/Shutterstock.com, 51; Keith Publicover/Shutterstock.com, 64; Ragnar Schmuck/Getty Images, 74; JGI/Blend Images/Getty Images, 89; Tony Hallas/Science Faction/Getty Images, 100; © WorldPhotos/Alamy Stock Photo, 105; Black Rock Digital/Shutterstock.com, 107; Selimaksan/ Getty Images, 118.

Printed in the United States of America

TABLE OF CONTENTS

You are the queen (or king) of your own imagination.
There you can engage and explore all the wonders
of math.

INTRODUCTION

As you head into this book, I want you to hold two ideas in your mind: 1) I want you to pretend that ideas and equations are interesting and sparkly. 2) I want you to pretend that you are capable of more than people around you seem to think that you are. Just try it. Test it out like an experiment. Going in, you are perfectly free to be skeptical about how it will turn out. I mean that. Pretending means you act and say things to yourself *as if* you were putting on a play about someone who agrees with those two ideas. If you just pretend, then you've been more than fair to my experiment.

How can math be *that* interesting? Well, let me be honest. It might not be. It's a real experiment, and when you get to the end of it, it might turn out that you still didn't stumble on any cool ideas or examples that changed your mind about it. I am perfectly good with that. Here's what I'm not OK with: you thinking that math is too boring or too hard or too **snarkleous** *just because someone else told you it was.* I don't know what "snarkleous" means. I just made it up. Have it stand for whatever other idea you have about how math is too _____. And sometimes people don't even have to bad-mouth math. Sometimes it's just the way they act about it. So? That's them. Are you allowed to like different stuff? Are they totally wrong about stuff sometimes? How do you know this isn't one of those times?

Put your seatbelt on, because I'm going to tell you something else you might not expect to hear from someone who is a parent, a teacher, a math lover, or all three: sometimes parents and teachers are as wrong as your friends. Sometimes parents and teachers act like math is too lame or too hard or too snarkleous. Don't believe them. Chances are the only reason they bought into that was because their friends or teachers sold them on the idea, and they held on to it.

So, hey, not a bad start to a math book, right? Sometimes you're the smartest. Sometimes you should test out an idea for yourself.

Here's the other part. Sometimes what they (friends, teachers, parents) are wrong about is what your mind is capable of understanding, or how well you're able to stick with something even if it's hard or confusing at first. So what if you have to read a section of the book two or three times so that it makes sense to you? Tons of the people you think are crazy smart have done that. Often. Then, once it does make sense, you will be even smarter and more awesome. Do you think famous singers and athletes and movie directors just came home from the hospital that awesome after they were born? I promise, they tested the experiment for themselves—they pretended they might be awesome, and then ran with it and found out they actually were awesome afterward.

So come with me to explore the interesting, sparkly world of mathematical **functions**. Together, let's find out the results of your experiment.

ONE

The History of Functions

The development of the contemporary field of functions is a different sort of story than we would find in tracing the development of other areas of mathematics like geometry or algebra. The reason it is different is that it was not quite all one field at first. As the pieces developed, only gradually did the great historical minds realize that when they were tangled together they would allow for some additional problem solving.

Before we move into a consideration of the historic development, though, it will be helpful to understand what we really mean by a function and, in particular, what we mean by a "transcendental function." In the process, we will also have a better understanding of why functions did not emerge from within the development of algebra or geometry.

Two key ideas will get us up and running with a sense of what kind of tools are being added to our toolbox. The first of these ideas is a rather simple one: What is a function?

"Function" is a term that refers to a mathematical operation that takes in different possible values of x and assigns to each x a single y value. Let's talk about some examples to see what we mean. We can think of a mathematical function as a kind of small machine. We put some pieces in, and it smooshes them together, chops them into smaller pieces, squashes them down to smaller size, or stretches them out to make them bigger. If we have a function like $y = 2x$, then any time we put a value in one end, that little machine stretches it out and puffs it up to make it bigger than it was before—put in a 7, we get out a 14.

Sometimes the math machines give us two things back instead of one. When working with graphs of functions, it's a quick, easy test to imagine to yourself: if I chopped this graph straight down with a big samurai sword, would it cut the graph in more than one place? If the answer is yes, it isn't a function. Functions can only have one y value for each x. How would that work if you graphed $x = y^2 + 4$? What about $y = 0x$? How about $0x = y^2 + 4$? Think carefully. Only one of those is a function!

Now for the second part: What makes some functions transcendental and some just regular?

There are two ingredients for being regular: a function has to be the result of using the four normal operations of arithmetic $(+, -, \times, \div)$, and it has to be the result of doing them some finite number of times. But this isn't true for transcendental functions. In fact, you might remember talking about transcendental numbers at some point along the way, and this is similar. With transcendental numbers, there is no finite number of steps that would ever finish calculating one of those numbers—like π. As long as we (or the computer) keep on performing the operation, we're going to keep on getting out more numbers to add to the tail end. The same is true with an operation like e^x. So, "transcendental" is kind of another way of saying "non-regular." In this case we say "non-algebraic."

I think we're ready to head out now. Let's look at three different developments that fall into this category of non-algebraic functions: trigonometric functions, **exponential** functions, and logarithmic functions.

Trigonometry

Since trigonometry is the oldest of the group and the one that has ended up being kind of the backbone of the modern area of functions, let's work from there and build onto it.

The term itself comes from ancient Greek words for "triangle" (*trigonon*) and for "measure" (*metron*). For most of the history of the study, trigonometry focused on the different ways to figure out the missing measurement for a triangle if other pieces were known. This helped not just with things that were specifically triangle-shaped, but with things that could be broken into triangles as well. While it primarily developed out from geometry, trig (as it is commonly called) had a different personality from the rest of geometry. For the Greeks and other ancients, geometry was about comparing sizes and **proportions**, whereas trig was more focused on figuring out the numbers.

The Mediterranean region

It is hard to pin down exactly who had trig first or most. There were a number of countries that had developed rudimentary versions of key concepts in response to certain real-world puzzles they needed to be able to solve. These included the big goals of any civilized civilization. Trigonometry exists in archaeological artifacts like the Rhind papyrus, dating to as far back as 1800 BCE. You might not recognize the terms, but by showing how they were used—like helping measure and build the pyramids—the papyrus has allowed scholars to figure out that they are often concepts and operations we still use.

An important thinker in the history of trig was Hipparchus, who was born around 190 BCE. Among his accomplishments was

Ptolemy, the Greek astronomer, made observations and measurements of the moon and stars.

creating the first chart for trig functions. (Seriously, who wants to re-calculate those for quantities you use often?) He did some great work, though it was still couched in geometric terms/forms that would be such a sharp contrast to later developments.

Ptolemy's book *Almagest* was the first of the ancient books about trig that filtered into Europe. This thirteen-volume astronomy text was *the* textbook up until the time of Copernicus. In addition to this massive work, he is known to have produced others as well, but we don't know much about him or his life besides that.

India and the Middle East

Our modern use of the 360 degree system came from the Indian scholars in trig, and the process of connecting Ptolemy's proportions to numeric relationships was a valuable step forward. Indian mathematicians transformed one of Ptolemy's ideas into the modern version of the **sine**, and one of the first tables of sines was in a book called the *Aryabhattva*.

It is also worth noting that some of our modern trig terms came about as a result of translations of Greek into Indian, Indian to Arabic, and then Arabic to Latin. Unless history of vocabulary is one of the few of your favorite things, there's no need to dig through all that. (Feel free to take a *Sound of Music* dance break; I'll be here when you get back.)

When most of Europe was going through the Dark Ages, it was Jewish and Muslim scholars who kept math (and science) moving forward. Accomplishments worth mentioning during this era include the first table of tangents and cotangents. Also, a clever Arabic astronomer named al-Battani came up with a rule for using shadows as a way to calculate the elevation of the sun above the horizon—an angle we know as θ.

Exponential Functions

This can be a little confusing because there have been exponents since the days of ancient Greece, and some of their rules have been developed and used for the centuries since. But we're specifically talking about *exponential functions*. The best way to understand the difference between a regular function and an exponential function is to offer two different cases and talk about why they're similar and different.

Regular function with exponents in it:

$$f(x) = 5x^2$$

Exponential function:

$$f(x) = 5a^x$$

With equations having the generalized form $y = a^x$, what happens is that the amount it changes by each time (x) depends on how much was already there (a). For example, how much mold will grow in the next hour/day/week depends on how much there already is. We are not changing *which* number gets multiplied by itself, as we are in the above example of a regular function. We're changing *how many* times a number gets multiplied by itself.

Among exponential functions, e^x is considered the most important because it is often the clearest example of the effect. This function is woven into the rate of growth and death of natural organisms. Interestingly enough, however, it was not the study of natural systems that led Jakob Bernoulli to recognize the potential impact of e. Instead, he was in the process of trying to understand compound interest, a man-made phenomenon. It has only been in the time since his work in 1683 that we have found it to be a fitting piece of the puzzle in projects from the decay of plutonium molecules to the explosive growth of mold colonies and the human population.

Logarithms

As interesting as this idea from Jakob Bernoulli's thinking was, an even more interesting idea came from John Napier. Napier was born in 1550 in Scotland. Sometimes in math, what you really need is not a way to do something but a way to undo something. In the process of undoing, you might discover a knot or some pieces of machinery that are fused together. When Napier figured out a great shortcut tool for doing big, ugly multiplication problems, the process of working with them revealed an interesting ability to undo exponents as well.

Napier's big idea was published in 1614. As a simple example to illustrate how the use of logarithms can make math with large numbers easier, imagine that in the process of your work on a financial model, you find yourself confronted with the problem of 32,768 × 2,048. You could, of course, slowly churn your way through the problem, hoping not to make a mistake while doing it by hand. However, if we look up those numbers, we find that they are 2^{15} and 2^{11}. Now we're in luck because we can quickly solve $2^{15} \times 2^{11}$ by

Napier the wizard

John Napier was a wealthy Scottish landowner who spent most of his time hidden away in his castle. Nicknamed Marvelous Merchiston (Merchiston is where his family castle was), and referred to as a modern Archimedes, Napier liked to help fuel the local stories that he was a wizard. He would hardly be seen outside the castle without a long, black coat and a weird, black rooster.

One story is told that he confronted his servants over a theft. He placed the rooster in a dark toolshed. He told his servants that whoever the guilty person was, when he or she petted the rooster (who was covered in soot), his or her hand would be marked. When one of the servants came out with clean hands, Napier knew that guy had refused to pet the rooster, thus busting himself!

In addition to his insightful developments in math, Napier also managed to come up with an ingenious little gadget for running multiplication and division calculations—called Napier's bones. It worked by putting different rods (four-sided wooden pieces with a column of numbers carved on each side) in order and then running simple arithmetic operations on the resulting arrangement.

His castle is now part of Napier University in Edinburgh.

simply adding the exponents (since they have the same base): 2^{26}. What if the problem were 2,097,152 × 65,536? Those numbers are also base 2, but you can puzzle them out for yourself.

Napier's system was a little cumbersome, as he used the number 0.9999999 (also written as $1 - 10^{-7}$) as his base. Fortunately for all of us, his longtime collaborator, an English mathematician named Henry Briggs, had the idea of base 10. So, $\log_{10} 100 = 2$. That's another way of writing $10^2 = 100$.

Of course, not everything works out quite so simply. What happens if we are looking for log 2,345? That is not a sweet, round result of 10 with some integer as an exponent. The shortcut, then, needed a huge list or table so people could look up to see that the exponents would be. If I wanted the answer to log 2,345, I would look it up in a book—the first of which was published by Briggs in 1624 (Napier had passed away in 1617).

This process saved so much time that it continued to be used almost as much as we use calculators now. Briggs's reference book had calculated the numbers out to fourteen decimal places for all the numbers going from 1 to 20,000 and from 90,000 to 100,000. Briggs and another guy, Vlacq, worked to set up tables for trigonometry, too, calculating out the logs for each one-hundredth of a degree.

This way of framing and solving problems was a huge time saver and probably saved a ridiculous number of mathematicians and scientists from waking up at night with hand cramps (or brain cramps!) from doing all that calculation the long way. By the end of the book, as we have walked through a number of problems that use logarithms to untangle exponents, you will have a better sense of their importance and value.

So, enough talking about people from a long time ago. Let's start digging around to see how these different mathematical tools actually help build things, solve things, earn big piles of money, and generally make the world a shinier, more awesome place.

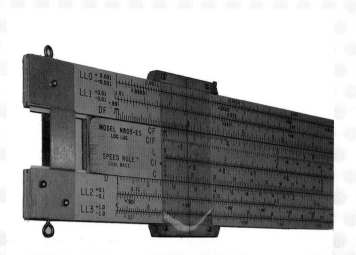

The slide rule

The slide rule is such a clever calculating device that until the advent of the modern calculator, it was practically part of the hand of practicing mathematicians and engineers into the 1950s and '60s. With the rise of calculators and computers, it finally became obsolete in the 1970s.

It looks like two rulers, one fitting into a wide groove along the length of the other one, and the edges of both are marked. It was invented in the seventeenth century by Reverend William Oughtred (with ideas from some others) in order to work more easily with the logarithms being developed by Napier and Briggs.

By understanding how to break complex math problems down-into **component** pieces, the scientist or engineer could use the slide rule to perform operations on those component pieces and then put them back together. As they developed over time, slide rules would allow for processing multiplication, division, square roots, exponents, logarithms, and trigonometric functions.

It is easy to look at something like this from our vantage point and think, "Oh, what an interesting, old-fashioned kind of gadget." We should consider, however, that we got people into space and landed them on the moon using slide rules. In fact, the story goes that Buzz Aldrin grabbed his for a couple of last-minute calculations before touching down.

TWO

Functions in Your Everyday Life

I n this chapter, we will tour some of the cool ways that functions can help us make sense of the different things in the world around us, as well as a few of the different things inside us! The most important thing I would mention is to not be in a hurry. Like watching butterflies unfold their wings or a nice, fat snowball exploding in slow-motion against your friend's chest, you will miss some cool things if you hurry. What is more, you won't understand what you just glanced at, so you will not be any more amazed or any more clever than you were when you picked up the book.

The Squishy Machine

I thought it would be fun to start out this time with some samples of the mathematics going on in this squishy system we drive around every day—the human body.

Blood of kings

Did you know that you are probably descended from Charlemagne, the great emperor of the Holy Roman Empire? (OK, everyone who just sat up a little taller, raise your hands.) This is kind of a fun puzzle to experiment

Charlemagne became the first Holy Roman emperor in 800 CE.
Mathematical functions can help show how you might be related to him.

with, so let's just walk through a basic version so you will get the spirit of it.

We have to start by setting up some basic, reasonable estimates for a few things. You can go back through and plug in other options later to see how the outcomes would shift. So let's start with dear, dear Karl der Grosse. (France and Germany weren't separate kingdoms yet, so that's his name in German. In Latin he was Carolus Magnus.) Charlemagne sounds a little less like a mean-spirited playground comment, so maybe we should stick with that. Charlemagne was born in about 745 CE and he and his first wife started having children in 767 CE when Big C was twenty-two years old—we'll round that to twenty.

Let's just imagine that they had two kids who grew up and had two kids, and so on, and so on. Some had more than two, but there were lots of wars and diseases and dinosaurs and stuff running loose, so not everyone survived long enough to have children. You get the idea. (No, there weren't still dinosaurs. The unicorns had chased them away by then.) We can plug this into an equation, then, to see how many descendants of Charlemagne there would have been, say, five generations on (a nice hundred-year figure).

$$D_c = 2^{(Y_n - Y_c)/20}$$

where:

D_c = Descendants of Charlemagne.
Y_n = The year that is being considered.
Y_c = The year Charlemagne was born.

A quick test shows that by the time Charlemagne was twenty, he had two kids:

$$D_c = 2^{20/20}$$

$$= 2^1$$

$$= 2$$

And what if we look a hundred years after he was born?

$$D_c = 2^{100/20}$$

$$= 2^5$$

$$= 32$$

Not bad. He would have had four grandkids, eight great-grandkids, sixteen great-great grandkids, and thirty-two great-great-great-grandkids. That was just a warm up, though! What happens when we get to 1745, when it's been one thousand years?

$$D_c = 2^{1000/20}$$
$$= 2^{50}$$
$$= 1,125,900,000,000,000$$

That's one million billion. (You can see why they gave up on sending each other birthday cards!)

Of course, in the whole world in 1765, there were only about a billion people on the planet, and we can be sure that at least a few of those were not descended from Charlemagne (none of the Native Americans, for instance!). So we can appreciate that the number shrinks down considerably. Many paths of heredity don't end up with that many separate individuals, but instead you have people who have, say, a bunch of their great-grandparents who were also descended from Charlemagne.

We could add a lot of extra research and complicating details, like exact likelihoods of getting killed off in wars, plagues, trampled by students on the way to recess, and so on. Mathematicians estimate that by now almost everyone whose ancestors married someone from Europe and suddenly had a family-sized grocery bill is incredibly likely to be descended at least partly from Charlemagne. See if you can guess how many people alive today with Europeans sitting in the branches of their family tree are also descended from lots of other great kings and queens and counts and empresses of Europe. If you have no Europeans in your family tree, no sweat, you will be descended from other great kings and queens and emperors and princesses from other parts of the world!

But, hey, all that wondrous and noble blood doesn't just sit around in your system telling everyone else what to do. It pumps around in time to some cool mathematical principles.

You don't actually have just one blood pressure all day long. Even on days when you don't exercise, the measurements will change in a regular up-and-down cycle. That means we can probably understand it by seeing which of the cyclic functions it most resembles! (Yay! Cut to random scenes of cheering crowds from different movies and TV shows!) The **coefficients** will vary somewhat from person to person. In this case, the equation is:

$$B_t = 80 + 7 \times \sin(\pi t/12)$$

where:

B_t = Blood pressure at time t.
t = Hours since midnight.
π = That circle thing (if you've forgotten, it is a magical unending number that represents the relationship between the diameter of a circle and its circumference).

At noon, then, we would see a **diastolic** pressure of:

$$B_t = 80 + 7 \times \sin(\pi t/12)$$
$$= 80 + 7 \times \sin(\pi \times 12/12)$$
$$= 80 + 7 \times \sin(\pi)$$
$$= 80 + 7 \times 0$$
$$= 80$$

In contrast, at 6 p.m., we would see:

$$B_t = 80 + 7 \times \sin(\pi t/12)$$
$$= 80 + 7 \times \sin(\pi \times 18/12)$$

$$= 80 + 7 \times \sin(1.5\pi)$$
$$= 80 + 7 \times -1$$
$$= 80 - 7$$
$$= 73$$

Kind of interesting, right? Your blood pressure doesn't just follow a cycle over the course of the day. It also follows a cycle in relation to your heartbeat. If you think about that for a second, why shouldn't it? Your heart moves in a cycle. Naturally, the pressure exerted each time your heart contracts would increase and then decrease. The high and low pressures are called **systolic** and diastolic. (Here's a way to remember: *di*astolic is when the heart *di*lates, or opens bigger, like your pupils when someone turns the light off or when you're thinking.)

So, again allowing that each person's equation would be a little different, let's consider the function that models one person's blood pressure:

$$B_t = 115 + 25 \times \sin(160\pi t)$$

where:

B_t = Blood pressure at time t.
t = Time in minutes.

The value of a sine wave goes from 1 at the top of its cycle to −1 at the bottom of its cycle. Therefore, at some point $\sin(160\pi t)$ will equal 1, and another point it will equal −1. So the different pressures will range from:

$$B_t = 115 + 25 \times 1 = 140$$

Trigonometry helps us understand the way our blood pressure goes up and down all the time.

$$B_t = 115 + 25 \times -1 = 90$$

That gives us blood pressure of 140/90, which is a little higher than normal (around 120/80).

A lot of that blood pumping through the body is to help feed our amazing brains, like when we are working to learn something. In fact, that blood arrives when we are trying to learn something about what happens when we are trying to learn something. (Stay with me, it will untangle in a minute.)

The process of learning new things follows an exponential growth curve, called a "learning curve." It shows the rate some output improves as a result of increasing the inputs. In most cases, the curve climbs less and less with each additional input and may even start to go back down at some overload point.

Let's consider an example of an athlete training for the high jump. A general form for such an equation would be:

$$H_t = M - Ce^{-0.025t}$$

where:

H_t = The height of his high jump after t months of practice.
M = Some predetermined **maximum** height he is aiming for.
C = A constant.
t = Time in months.

In this example, let's have a new athlete training for the high jump. We'll plug in the Olympic record of 2.54 meters. If the coach has been tracking the athlete's data and feeds it in, the computer gives the following equation for the athlete aiming just above that record:

$$H_t = 2.55 - 1.5e^{-0.025t}$$

How many months will it take him to achieve a height of 2 meters?

$$2.0 = 2.55 - 1.5e^{-0.025t}$$

Let's get the e term by itself by subtracting 2.55 from both sides:

$$-0.55 = -1.5e^{-0.025t}$$

Divide both sides by −1.5:

$$0.367 = e^{-0.025t}$$

Your own computer

To get a real appreciation for the squishy machine, let's take a few minutes to reflect on our most complex organ: the brain. The average human brain contains about one hundred billion neurons—the microscopic nerve cells that make up our computer. That's about the same as the number of stars in our Milky Way galaxy, and if you counted one every second, it would take 3,171 years. These neurons can each be connected to up to ten thousand other neurons. That means the electric signals in the brain are zooming around on a highway system (at speeds over 2,000 miles per hour, or 3,220 kilometers per hour) with about one thousand trillion roads in it. That is the equivalent of the number of stars in ten thousand galaxies like ours. Yet the total electricity only adds up to a low-watt light bulb.

On top of that, your brain also has about a trillion glial cells. They help the neurons in a variety of ways, including rebuilding and rewiring connections. And let's not forget the 400 miles (650 kilometers) of blood vessels folded up in there, too! Maybe we shouldn't be surprised that some experts think we have as many as seventy thousand thoughts per day.

Even better, learning that new information probably just helped build some new pathways!

To undo e to some power, we take the natural log of both sides. The natural log is just a logarithm with a base of e.

$$\ln 0.367 = -0.025t$$

Divide both sides by -0.025:

$$\ln 0.367/-0.025 = t$$
$$40.09 = t$$

It will take just over 40 months for the athlete to reach 2 meters.

Sadly, though, our brain does not just work in one direction. It is also designed to erase information over time. Of course, that seems unhelpful, since it might get rid of information that we need, but in general, the process of constantly clearing stuff out frees up room, which we need. You can think of it as sending your robo-vac to clean your room every week. It's useful and saves you immense amounts of time doing it. Of course, it might not realize that some of the stuff on the floor you would have wanted to keep.

In contrast to a learning equation, then, we have a forgetting equation. This can be shown as:

$$\log S_t = \log S_0 - c \times \log(t + 1)$$

where:

S = Your score on the science test.
t = Some length of time.
c = A constant representing the rate you tend to forget stuff.

If your normal rate of forgetting stuff tends to be, say, 0.15 per month, then if we compared your science test results of 95 percent today to your score on the same test five months from now, how would we predict you would do?

$$\log S_t = \log S_0 - c \times \log(t + 1)$$

First, let's simplify this down a bit using some log rules. We can move the constant up to an exponent:

$$\log S_t = \log S_0 - \log(t + 1)^c$$

Then we can condense the right side.

$$\log S_t = \log[S_0/(t + 1)^c]$$

We can kill off the "logs" since they're the same on both sides:

$$S_t = S_0/(t + 1)^c$$

Now we put in some information from the problem:

$$S_t = 95/(5 + 1)^{0.15}$$

Then crunch it down:

$$S_t = 95/6^{0.15}$$
$$S_t = 95/1.30835$$
$$S_t = 72.6$$

Ouch. Hardly seems fair after you worked so hard for that 95, does it? The trade-off is that refreshing something you've already learned results in a much faster learning curve the second time. In a way, you've done a bunch of training to get ready for ramping up when you need that information more often.

Flow rates

There are two functions, one for blood and one for nerve impulses, that you might expect to behave on similar patterns. When nerve impulses are zipping around carrying messages back and forth to the brain and the spinal cord, their speed is in direct proportion to the diameter of the fiber along which they are traveling. Knowing that about them, and given that a nerve impulse can travel at 40 meters per second along a fiber that is 6 **micrometers** thick, how fast would we expect impulses to zoom along an 8 micrometer fiber?

$$\frac{6 \text{ micrometers}}{40 \text{ sec}} = \frac{8 \text{ micrometers}}{x \text{ m/sec}}$$

$$(8 \times 40)/6 = 53.33$$

We'd expect the impulses to move at more than 53 m/sec.

In contrast, the resistance to the flow of blood through a vessel is **inversely** proportional to the blood vessel's radius to the fourth power. What we mean here is:

$$y = \frac{k}{x^n}$$

In this case, for example,

$$R = \frac{kl}{r^4}$$

where:

R = The resistance to blood flow.
k = A constant.
l = The length of the blood vessel in centimeters.
r = The radius of the blood vessel in millimeters.

Let's assume we have a blood vessel that's 12 centimeters long and has a radius of 0.2 millimeters. The resistance is measured in mmHg, or millimeters of mercury, the standard for blood pressure. Let's say it's 25. So, we need to find k:

$$25 = \frac{12k}{0.2^4} = \frac{12k}{0.0016}$$

$$25 \times 0.0016 = 12k$$

$$0.04 = 12k$$

$$k = \frac{1}{300}$$

Now we substitute k back into the original equation:

$$R = \frac{1}{300} \times \frac{12}{r^4}$$

What happens if the blood moves to a slightly larger vessel? Let's give a new radius of 0.3 mm:

$$R = \frac{1}{300} \times \frac{12}{0.3^4}$$

$$R = \frac{12}{2.43} = 4.94 \text{ mmHg}$$

That small change in radius dramatically reduces the pressure of the flow. If you have ever put your thumb over the end of your garden hose to make the water spray farther, you will get the idea here.

Populations

It should come as no surprise that our brains and bodies are hardly the only natural systems that seem to be programmed with math codes. We see this holding true in the case of things on the tiny scale, like colonies of bacteria. One of the key features of different kinds of bacteria is their rate of growth (which is directly tied to their rate of consumption) and how quickly they are able to break down nutrients and cycle them back into the nutrient cycle.

Let's look at one kind of bacteria, for instance, that has a division cycle of four hours. We want to find out how many hours it would take for a group of 100 bacteria to grow to some population size P. This is represented by the equation:

$$t = 4 \times \frac{\log\left(\frac{P}{100}\right)}{\log 2}$$

If we wanted to see how long it would take for the population to spread to, say, a million bacteria, we plug in the number 1,000,000 for P and work it out:

$$t = 4 \times \frac{\log\left(\frac{1,000,000}{100}\right)}{\log 2}$$

$$t = 4 \times \frac{\log(10,000)}{\log 2}$$

$$t = 4 \times \frac{4}{0.30103}$$

$$= 4 \times 13.28771$$

$$= 53.15 \text{ hours}$$

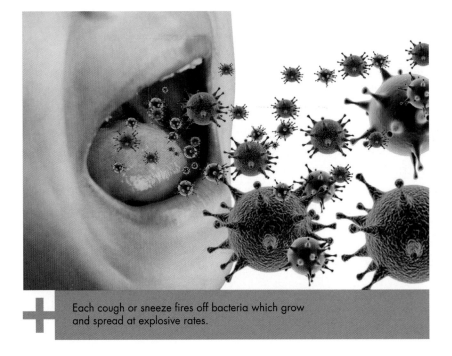

Each cough or sneeze fires off bacteria which grow and spread at explosive rates.

Take a second and think about what this kind of growth actually means. It means that in just four more hours, the colony will be at two million, and within a day, it will reach a total of sixty-four million. Well, don't freak out just yet. A tiny pinch of soil can hold forty million bacteria, and a kiss is going to involve about eighty million. (I know, right?) Seriously, though, they're not all bad. There are about a thousand different kinds of bacteria living in our intestines, and the population reaches into the trillions. There are more bacteria in our intestines than there are cells in our body, but without these, you would not be able to digest food or fight off the harmful stuff that manages to make its way into our digestive tract.

Part of what is interesting, though, is that these mathematical models apply at the large scale as well as the small, and everything from rabbits to rhinoceroses can be modeled in a similar way—just as long as we adjust the rates and exponents appropriately.

In the case of humans, the equation would look more like:

$$P_t = P_0 e^{rt}$$

where:

P_t = Population at t.
P_0 = Population now.
r = Rate of population growth.
t = Number of years from now.

Our current world population is about 7.4 billion people. Thankfully, we don't double every four hours like bacteria. It's 2016 at the time of writing, and our growth rate per year for the last couple years has been around 1.13 percent per year. With those numbers, we can drop them into the equation and see what the world population will be by 2030.

$$P_t = 7.4e^{0.0113 \times 14}$$

Multiply our exponent elements:

$$P_t = 7.4e^{0.15820}$$

Calculate the e part:

$$P_t = 7.4 \times 1.1714$$
$$P_t = 8.67 \text{ billion people}$$

However, within fifty years from now—probably the time of your grandchildren (also descended from royalty, of course!)—the population of humans on Earth would be:

$$P_t = 7.4e^{0.0113 \times 50}$$

$$P_t = 7.4e^{0.565}$$

$$P_t = 7.4 \times 1.7595$$

$$P_t = 13.02 \text{ billion people}$$

That is humongous.

Well, someplace like New York City has a population density of just a smidge under twenty-eight thousand people per 1 square mile (2.6 square kilomters), so that would mean all the people in the world could fit in a city like New York if it were as big as 465,000 square miles (1.2 million sq km). It's hard to get our brains around a number like that. As it turns out, New York City is 468 square miles (1,212 sq km) in size, which works out conveniently for a little mental math—in 2050, everyone would fit in one thousand cities like New York City. (If we scrunched into just one thousand cities, that is. I'm not saying it would be fun.)

I'm afraid that still doesn't really relate for most of us. It seems huge, but that's because there's no context. (Remember how you thought briefly about freaking out over all those bacteria running rampant just a few minutes ago?)

To give us a sense of scale, then, Texas is 268,000 square miles (694,100 sq km), so two of those would do it. It's still not a meaningful picture, though. Let's really put it into scale: if we rule out deserts and stuff, there are about 24.6 million square miles (63.7 million sq km) of habitable land on the planet. That means all the people, in theory, could live in about 1/52nd of the total, or about 2 percent. Closer to useful. It's still a little off, because we would need to factor in some extra space for landfills, fuel processing, lumber resources, and so on. Even if we double it, the space is not a freak-out factor yet. We'll revisit this in a little while.

Human populations, like New York City, expand in a similar way to bacteria (though more slowly, thankfully).

In the meantime, let's talk about a few other areas of nature where the functions function. Not only populations follow these rules, but individual things also have mathematical equations that represent their growth. Consider trees, for example. Their patterns of growth waver from the curve depending on certain factors from year to year, but over time, we can model their growth rates with an equation. One equation for a species of tree could look like this:

$$D_t = \frac{5.3}{1 + 2.8e^{-0.01t}}$$

where:

D_t = Diameter of the tree in feet.
t = Time in years.

Notice the negative exponent on the e. That tells us that as time goes on, the extra growth each year is a smaller and smaller amount. This is true of many organisms. Babies grow like crazy from year 1 to year 2, but not a lot of growth spurts happen between year 48 and 49.

For our tree, then, we could plug in year 2 and year 5 to see how much it has grown, and then we'll contrast that with the change from year 400 to year 403.

In year 2:

$$D_t = \frac{5.3}{1 + 2.8e^{-0.01 \times 2}} = \frac{5.3}{1 + 2.8e^{-0.02}} = \frac{5.3}{1 + (2.8 \times 0.98)}$$

$$= \frac{5.3}{1 + 2.74} = \frac{5.3}{3.74} = 1.417 \text{ feet}$$

In year 5:

$$D_t = \frac{5.3}{1 + 2.8e^{-0.01 \times 5}} = \frac{5.3}{1 + 2.8e^{-0.05}} = \frac{5.3}{1 + (2.8 \times 0.95)}$$

$$= \frac{5.3}{1 + 2.66} = \frac{5.3}{3.66} = 1.45 \text{ feet}$$

In year 400:

$$D_t = \frac{5.3}{1 + 2.8e^{-0.01 \times 400}} = \frac{5.3}{1 + 2.8e^{-4}} = \frac{5.3}{1 + (2.8 \times 0.183)}$$

$$= \frac{5.3}{1 + 0.0513} = \frac{5.3}{1.0513} = 5.04 \text{ feet}$$

In year 403:

$$D_t = \frac{5.3}{1 + 2.8e^{-0.01 \times 403}} = \frac{5.3}{1 + 2.8e^{-4.03}} = \frac{5.3}{1 + (2.8 \times 0.178)}$$

$$= \frac{5.3}{1 + 0.0498} = \frac{5.3}{1.0498} = 5.049 \text{ feet}$$

So the average yearly difference in the early three years is 0.011 feet (3.35 millimeters) per year, while the average yearly difference in the later years is 0.00267 feet (0.8 mm) per year. That's down to 25 percent of what it was early on.

Interestingly enough, there are also ways to use logarithmic functions to help estimate age for wild things that are not as easy to sneak up on and measure as trees are. For example, the age of female blue whales can be estimated using:

$$t = -2.57 \times \ln\left(\frac{87 - L}{63}\right)$$

where:

t = Age in years.
L = Length in feet.

If researchers spot an 80-foot-long female, they would record her age in the field log as:

$$t = -2.57 \times \ln\left(\frac{87 - 80}{63}\right)$$

$$t = -2.57 \times \ln\left(\frac{7}{63}\right)$$

$$t = -2.57 \times \ln\left(\frac{1}{9}\right)$$

$$t = -2.57 \times -2.197 = 5.6 \text{ years old}$$

Death rates for a given species and population also follow curves we can map out. In these examples, so far we have been looking at populations by themselves. A more realistic treatment needs to account for dangers in the environment, like the large number of things that think you might be edible. As you might guess, the populations of predators and their prey follow an up and down cycle. One example of such a cycle might be where the number of predators increases. They eat up a large population of their prey, and then the predators die down due to food shortages. This means the prey is able to grow in population numbers again, and back and forth. An example of such a relationship can be represented by:

$$P_p = 900 \times \cos(2t) + 8{,}000$$

where:

P_p = Population of prey.
t = Number of years.

Since we know the cycle of **cosine** can vary from −1 to 1, we can see that the population of prey animals would cycle from 7,100 at a low point up to 8,900 at a high point. That might not seem like that many, but consider that is an average level of 8,000 that bounces up and down by a little over 10 percent. You will notice that the population cycle of the predators is very dependent on the prey, but is not the same ratio at each level. On row one, the ratio is 1.2 percent, while on row three—the low point—it is 1.0 percent. The change in numbers there seems small, but the difference between 1.2 and 1.0 is about a 17 percent fluctuation. The change in available prey affects the consumption rate and the reproduction rate of the predators. The two populations move together.

Year	Prey	Predators
0	8,900	107
π/4 (0.78)	8,000	92
π/2 (1.57)	7,100	74
3π/4 (2.36)	8,000	92

A second element that allows us to map the functions onto a more realistic model is to relate them to the context of an ecosystem where animals are not just trying to outrun their food or become food, but are also competing with other organisms for limited resources, like space, nutrients, and fresh water. The maximum population due to these limited resources is referred to as the "carrying capacity" of an area, and it has a dampening effect on those starry-eyed growth plans all those newlywed bacteria had for starting and raising large colonies of their own.

A growth model that takes the carrying capacity into account is called a logistic model, and it reduces the annual increase by factoring in how close the population is getting to that upper limit. A generalized equation would be:

$$P_t = \frac{m}{P_0 + 5.9e^{-0.02t}}$$

where:

P_t = The population at time t.
P_0 = The population at time 0.
m = A constant (the maximum potential capacity).
t = Time in years.

If we re-run the model on human population, then, we would find that the estimated population growth in the next fifty years will have gotten smaller and smaller as it approached the calculated carrying capacity. Compare this to our earlier model, which only took into account the space available:

$$P_t = \frac{73.3}{7.4 + 5.9e^{-0.02t}}$$

$$P_t = \frac{73.3}{7.4 + 5.9e^{-0.02 \times 50}} = \frac{73.3}{7.4 + 2.17} = \frac{73.3}{9.57}$$

$$= 7.66 \text{ billion, instead of } 13 \text{ billion}$$

Yay, we don't all have to move to New Yorks the size of Texas! (Can you imagine the noise? The traffic?)

Functions can model other aspects of natural groups, like migratory patterns. Migration is one way some species work to solve the problem of carrying capacity in a given area of their biome.

The population of one migratory species of birds might have a function like this (measured in hundreds):

$$P(t) = 60 + 60 \times \cos\left(\frac{\pi t}{6}\right)$$

where:

P = Population.
t = Time in months.

What are the maximum and **minimum** number of animals that would be spotted during the year at a certain checkpoint?

Since cosine can range over −1 to 1, the range would be from 0 to 12,000.

The final aspect to tie a lot of the pieces together is the complex model used to reflect the diversity of species that are part of an ecosystem. The name for this complex calculation is the index of diversity, and it looks like this:

$$H = -(P_1 \times \log_2 P_1 + P_2 \times \log_2 P_2 + \dots + P_n \times \log_2 P_n)$$

where:

$P_1, P_2, \dots, P_n$ = The proportion of a sample that belongs to each species (Species 1, Species 2, etc.).

For example, if we had a simple community of 100 members, made up of 80 members of one species and 20 members of another species:

$$P_1 \text{ would equal } \frac{80}{100} = 0.8$$

$$P_2 \text{ would equal } \frac{20}{100} = 0.2$$

We want to find $\log_2 0.8$ and $\log_2 0.2$. We can use the natural log function to make each more user-friendly:

$$\log_2 0.8 = \frac{\ln 0.8}{\ln 2} = -0.3219$$

$$\log_2 0.2 = \frac{\ln 0.2}{\ln 2} = -2.322$$

Now we plug those in to solve for H:

$$H = -(P_1 \times \log_2 P_1 + P_2 \times \log_2 P_2)$$
$$= -(0.8 \times -0.3219 + 0.2 \times -2.322)$$
$$= 0.722$$

Understanding the result of these diversity calculations changes depending on how many species are involved. In the case of just two species like this, an H value of 1 would mean they were distributed equally, and a rating closer to 0 would mean little or no diversity.

The Sound of Music

In addition to being used to perform the inverse function of exponentiation, logarithms are also a very useful tool for helping us to make sense out of numbers that have a crazy-wide range. Consider, for example, that the amount of energy unleashed by

The mathematical behavior of sound applies as much to whispers as to rock concerts and jet engines.

the largest earthquake on record was about one hundred billion times as much as for one of the earthquakes that can barely be felt. In order to work with numbers on that wide a range, our graphs and charts would be barely usable—either because they were so tall as to capture variance among the lower numbers, or because they would be scrunched to fit, in which case the smaller numbers wouldn't even be visible to the naked eye. (What good is a chart with invisible stuff on it?)

A similar principle applies in the case of decibels (named for Alexander Graham Bell, incidentally—deci*bel*s, see?). Consider:

Sound Intensity (watts/m²)	Sound
1.0×10^{-12}	Faintest sound most humans can hear
5.2×10^{-10}	Whisper
3.2×10^{-6}	Normal conversation
8.5×10^{-4}	Heavy traffic
8.3×10^{2}	Jet engine

That means the distance from a whisper to normal human conversation is four places. That's ten thousand times more intense. But why don't our ears fall off? Please don't misunderstand, here. We do not hear in logarithms. We just use logarithms to represent our hearing, so we don't have to make a chart that goes from 0 to 10,000. Keep in mind as we go forward that decibels do not tell you how much pressure is acting against your ears. They tell you how much *more* force *than* a whisper is pushing against your ear.

In order to calculate the decibels of normal conversation, we would start with:

$$D = 10 \times \log \frac{I}{I_0}$$

where:

D = Decibel measure.

I = The intensity of the sound being measured (in watts per square meter).

I_z = A standardized value for the quietest sound a person could hear.

$$D = 10 \times \log \frac{3.2 \times 10^{-6}}{1.0 \times 10^{-12}}$$

$$D = 10 \times \log (3.2 \times 10^{6})$$

$$D = 10 \times \log 3,200,000$$

$$D = 10 \times 6.50515$$

$$D = 65.05 \text{ decibels}$$

Dampening

In addition to the effects on your ears in terms of force, there are also some cool things going on within the different sounds themselves. Consider, for instance, the vibrations created by a violin string. This is an interesting case because it's not just a regular **frequency**, like your heartbeat or sunlight beaming down on us. Think about it: once you've plucked or bowed the violin string (or piano wire, or whatever) the sounds actually fades. That effect is called "dampening." Similar effects occur when you cause ripples in a pond or you bounce a ball—each time it gets shorter and shorter.

In the case of the violin string, a handy-dandy equation to represent this effect is:

$$y = ke^{-ct} \times \cos(\omega\pi t)$$

where:

k = The original distance of **displacement** (how far the string was pulled).
c = A dampening constant.
t = Time in seconds.
ω = The frequency (how long between repetition of the up and down wave cycle).

The frequency of the string is measured at 400 (a bit higher than the frequency of G above middle C). So, if we pull the string up 0.4 centimeters and then release it, we can model the **amplitude**—how far the plucked point travels above and below its initial resting place:

$$y = 0.4e^{-ct} \times \cos(400\pi t)$$

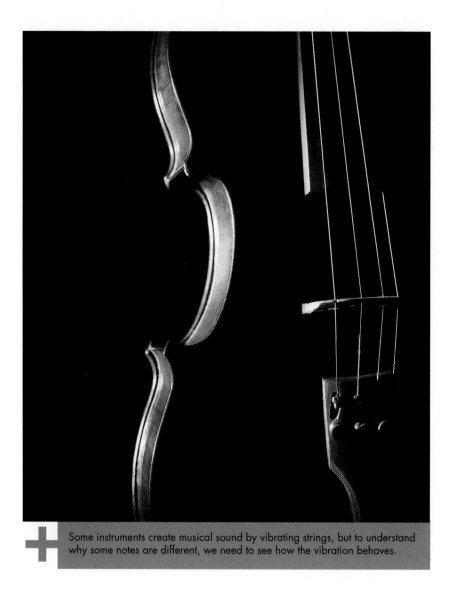

Some instruments create musical sound by vibrating strings, but to understand why some notes are different, we need to see how the vibration behaves.

At 1 second, then, we could calculate that the amplitude of the string's vibration is:

$$y = 0.4e^{-1.4 \times 1} \times \cos(400\pi \times 1)$$
$$y = 0.4e^{-1.4} \times \cos(400\pi)$$
$$y = 0.09864 \times \cos(400\pi)$$
$$y = 0.09864 \times 1 = 0.09864 \text{ centimeters}$$

But at 2 seconds, it has dropped to:

$$y = 0.4e^{-1.4 \times 2} \times \cos(400\pi \times 2)$$
$$y = 0.4e^{-2.8} \times \cos(800\pi)$$
$$y = 0.02432 \times \cos(800\pi)$$
$$y = 0.02432 \times 1 = 0.02432 \text{ centimeters}$$

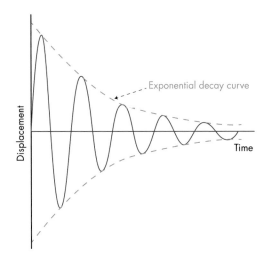

Not only is the sound getting smaller as the string's vibration fades, but there is also a softening effect on the musical note as it

Meet Rob Eckert

Please meet Rob Eckert, the bass guitarist for a young indie-rock band named Mead Lake's Most Wanted.

Thanks for hanging out for a bit, Rob. So, how long have you been doing music?

I've been playing different instruments and singing in school and out since about second grade (flutophones rule!). I picked up the bass guitar about five years ago when Mead Lake's Most Wanted formed.

What are some different kinds of math you use in composing, recording, and editing your songs?

Math is everywhere in music. The mix of measures and beats and time signatures affects how we put pieces together to make a musical line that either fits the rules in order to produce something that our brains are expecting, or breaks them to produce something unexpected.

One of the fun things about music is that we can make things work on different levels. Some artists go completely by feel, barely acknowledging the mathematics in the background. Others rely on them to help assemble their music or to communicate with others.

In Mead Lake's Most Wanted, we stay tuned from a mathematical standpoint, since we are not all lifelong musicians that are fluent in the feel of how to turn a blank page into a song.

Once something is there, we can tell if it's correct or incorrect, but being aware of the numbers and patterns under the surface allows us to move past that moment when we are all looking at each other thinking, "OK, what comes next in this song?"

From an engineering and equipment standpoint, probably the best example of having to use math to avoid a cataclysm is Ohm's law. String the wrong types of speakers together, and you will melt your amplifier and turn it into a very expensive, very heavy, somewhat smelly paperweight.

Is there a kind of math problem you work with that seems especially cool or different compared to what people usually think of as math?

In mixing music for the band, probably the most gratifying use of numbers is the display that is generated when illustrating frequency spectrums. It's essentially a chart that is plotted and re-plotted in real time, assigning different colors to frequencies that have varying intensities over time. This helps identify notes that are out of time, out of pitch, and that need equalization adjustment.

travels to your ear. The effect is called the inverse square law for sound. It basically says that the intensity of a sound is inversely proportional to the square of the distance from the source. This is a little mind-blowing because that means it works the same way gravitational attraction does. It just seems unreal to appreciate the idea that music would act like the force that pulls everything in the universe toward everything else.

Pressure

The reasoning behind why the sound gets softer by the time it gets to your ear is that sound comes from waves radiating outward in all directions, and some of them bump into your ears. The further the sound travels, the more air it has pushed into air that has pushed into air that … has pushed into the air inside your ears. (Think about how much easier it is to push a single grocery cart than it is to push fifty if they were all lined up.)

A trig function can show us how to model this weakening:

$$P = \frac{a}{r} \times \cos\left(\frac{2\pi r}{1} - ct\right)$$

where:

P = Sound pressure experienced.
r = Feet from the source.
l = Length of sound wave.
t = Time since the initial sound (seconds).
c = Speed of sound (feet per second).
a = Maximum sound pressure at the source (pounds per square foot).

If we let a = 3 lbs/ft², l = 4.9 ft, c = 1,026 ft/s, and t = 10 seconds, then how is pressure affected as r increases?

$$P = \frac{3}{r} \times \cos\left(\frac{2\pi r}{4.9} - 10{,}260\right)$$

Let's plug in 1 foot for *r*:

$$P = \frac{3}{1} \times \cos\left(\frac{2\pi \times 1}{4.9} - 10{,}260\right) = -0.4575 \text{ lbs/ft}^2$$

Let's plug in 6 feet for *r*:

$$P = \frac{3}{6} \times \cos\left(\frac{2\pi \times 6}{4.9} - 10{,}260\right) = -0.1388 \text{ lbs/ft}^2$$

Distance

Let's turn back to think about sound intensity in terms of decibels. The general formula for modeling this is:

$$I = \frac{k}{d^2}$$

where:

I = Intensity.
d = Distance from source of the sound.
k = A constant.

Recall our equation from above which calculated decibels. We can calculate the decibel difference of two intensities by slightly changing that equation:

$$D = 10 \times \log \frac{I_2}{I_1}$$

We get:

$$D = 10 \times \log \frac{\frac{k_2}{d_2}}{\frac{k_2}{d_1}}$$

$$D = 10 \times \log \left(\frac{d_1}{d_2}\right)^2$$

$$D = 2 \times 10 \times \log \left(\frac{d_1}{d_2}\right)$$

$$D = 20 \times \log \left(\frac{d_1}{d_2}\right)$$

That would mean at a rock concert, if we were getting blasted at 120 decibels sitting in the front row, about 2 meters away from the speakers, then moving back a few rows to get maybe 6 meters from the speakers would give us a reprieve of:

$$20 \times \log \left(\frac{2}{10}\right)$$

$$= 20 \times -0.69897$$

$$= -13.979$$

So we are brought from 120 decibels down to a survivable 106.02 decibels. Keep in mind: to our ear, that is several thousand times quieter.

Money

Let's examine the money machinery that makes the modern world click like clockwork. After all, things like going to rock concerts and even having a living room to sit in to listen to music depend on you being smart enough to manage your money and leverage it to make more money.

Perhaps the simplest and most familiar place to start is a savings account. It is a place where you stash your money to save up for things like your first home, launching your first business, or even getting a head start on plans for retiring early. As mentioned in chapter one, it is also one of the places where important, breakthrough ideas in math regarding the nature and shape of exponential growth happened.

Applying math to the different ways you can invest your money makes a big difference, so it should capture your interest. (Ha!)

Here's what happens in a bank: You put your money in. They then turn around and loan most of it out to other people—people buying their first home, people launching a new business, people making investments in projects and other companies and, interestingly enough, sometimes investing in other banks. They charge a certain percentage from the people they lend your money to, give you part of that percentage, and keep part of the percentage

Meet John Callen

This is John Callen, chief investment officer at Catholic Financial Life. He's been in that role for four years, but in various investment management roles for over twenty years.

Thanks for meeting with us, John. I'm guessing your job has a good healthy helping of math. Can you tell me a little about it?

Math is essential to my job because ultimately the results are measured in dollar values. I use sums, multiplication, exponential growth series, factoring, probabilities, and a broad array of statistical measures just about every day at work.

Why do you have to use them?

Investments are said to have a rate of return. You may have heard of interest rates. Interest rates are the percentage increase in value that investors receive over time through regular payments that we call interest income. You also know that some things increase in value over time because another investor is willing to pay you more for it than you paid for it yourself. This is called "appreciation" because the value appreciates, or increases, over time.

The safest investments have a steady rate of return. I need to project their values into the future to know if the insurance company will have enough money to pay money to our customers when bad things happen to them.

Other investments do not have a steady rate of return on investment. This uncertainty of return is called risk. Investors need to balance the likelihood and size of positive returns with the likelihood and size of negative returns to judge whether an investment risk is worth taking. My job is to limit the risk of disappointment to an acceptable level. Investment losses could force a business to fail.

Is there a kind of math problem or application that seems especially cool or different compared to "regular old stuff" you did in middle and high school?

Investment results in the future reflect all of the uncertainty that comes from not knowing what will happen in the future. There is one statistical exercise which tries to unravel whether an investment manager like myself is lucky or skilled compared to other investment managers. Another mathematical analysis attributes investment profits to various categories to help explain where results are coming from. I actually learned the analysis when I worked for a department store that wanted to know what stores had the best mix of sales and profits in each department!

for themselves. Let's say they loan it to a family buying their first home. The bank charges 5 percent and pays you 2 percent. The other 3 percent is the bank's profit from finding and organizing the borrowing and lending.

One of the reason the bank earns a profit is because it is taking a risk. If someone who borrowed money can't afford to pay it back, the bank still has to pay you for borrowing your money. That means the bank could be on the hook.

Because of that, your savings account is a pretty safe investment, but it also pays only a tiny percentage of interest every year. Let's see how your money works for you while you leave it in the bank. The equation for paying you interest is called the compound interest formula, and it looks like:

$$A = P \left(1 + \frac{i}{n}\right)^{nt}$$

where:

A = Your new balance after t years.
P = **Principal** (the original amount).
i = The annual interest rate the bank agrees to pay.
n = How many times per year they calculate and pay you interest on your account.
t = The number of years you leave money in your account collecting small but safe interest on it.

Let's say the bank is offering a 2 percent interest rate on savings accounts. If they just calculated and paid interest on your account, which contains $100,000, once each year, the math would be really easy: $100,000 × 0.02 = $2,000 each year.

Rather than calculate and pay out once per year, though, banks use compound interest. They run their numbers each month. So while they just say 2 percent, what they actually mean is "Hey, we'll run 2 percent as our annual rate and pay out each month."

So, your i is 2 percent, but your n is now 12, so the equation is starting to look like this:

$$A = P\left(1 + \frac{0.02}{12}\right)^{12t}$$

We said you were putting $100,000 in, and that's P.

$$A = 100{,}000 \times \left(1 + \frac{0.02}{12}\right)^{12t}$$

$$A = 100{,}000 \times (1 + 0.00167)^{12t}$$
$$A = 100{,}000 \times 1.00167^{12t}$$

And we'll just figure this out for one year, so $t = 1$:

$$A = 100{,}000 \times 1.00167^{12}$$
$$A = 100{,}000 \times 1.02018$$

See that extra little .018 on the end? That's from compounding.

$$A = \$102{,}018.43$$

With an extra $18 dollars a year, you're not quite on the fast track to early retirement. Hopefully, though, you're not saving up for just a year. Over ten years, your earnings will be:

$$A = 100{,}000 \times (1.00167)^{12\times10}$$
$$A = 100{,}000 \times 1.22169 = \$122{,}168.72$$

That's an average of 2.2 percent per year, instead of just 2 percent.

The kind of number I really want you to get your head around, though, is the difference you can make by starting early on your retirement savings. Let's jump ahead to when you are seventy-five. It's possible that will be the average age of retirement by the time you get there. If you put that $100,000 in the bank when you're twenty, then at the end of fifty-five years, it will add up to:

$$A = 100,000 \times (1.00167)^{12 \times 55} = \$300,801.58$$

If, instead, you wait until you're thirty to put the money in the bank to save for retirement:

$$A = 100,000 \times (1.00167)^{12 \times 45} = \$246,218.17$$

That means you lost out on an extra $54,583 that you could have accumulated. You just gave away $54,000. Granted, we might not all have $100,000 on hand that we can drop into an account, but notice the scale of impact holds: $246,218 is only 80 percent of $300,800. If anything, having a smaller amount to withdraw means the lost earnings would most likely affect us even more.

We can also, interestingly enough, use reasoning like we did with the growth of bacteria to ask how long it would take a given investment to double. Yes, I did compare money to bacteria. Isn't that an interesting metaphor?

Let's look at an investment of $5,000 and see how long it would take to get to $10,000 if we're earning 6 percent interest per year.

$$A = P\left(1 + \frac{0.06}{12}\right)^{12t}$$

$$A = \$5,000 \times 1.005^{12t}$$

Here we will go ahead and set A equal to $10,000 as the target:

$$\$10{,}000 = \$5{,}000 \times 1.005^{12t}$$

So we divide both sides by 5,000:

$$2 = 1.005^{12t}$$

To get that exponent down, we need to take the log of both sides:

$$\log 2 = \log(1.005)^{12t}$$

Now we can move the exponent down:

$$\log 2 = 12t \times \log(1.005)$$

Divide both sides by $12 \times \log(1.005)$:

$$\frac{\log 2}{12 \times \log 1.005} = t$$

$$\frac{0.30103}{0.02605} = t = 11.55 \text{ years}$$

A better option, however, is to start chipping money in each month to a retirement account. Two things happen to make more money. The first is that because you agree not to take the money out until you reach retirement age, the banks are willing to pay you a little bit more for using your money to loan to other people. The second is that by putting a little bit of money into the account each month, it adds up like you wouldn't believe. The equation for this kind of plan is a little bit different, because money keeps going in:

$$FV = Pmt \times \frac{\left(1 + \dfrac{r}{k}\right)^{nk} - 1}{\dfrac{r}{k}}$$

where:

FV = Future Value.
r = Annual interest rate.
k = Compounding periods per year.
n = Number of years.
Pmt = Amount you pay in each time. Let's use months here.

I know, it looks ugly and confusing. Be patient. Just think about one step at a time. This little piece of magic is one of the most powerful bits of math I could show you. This is the finance equivalent of the secret Shaolin technique for doing good things with your life.

So, let's say you put $100 every month into a plan from the time you are twenty until you are seventy. In that case, your earnings at a 6 percent annual interest rate would be:

$$FV = 100 \times \frac{\left(1 + \dfrac{0.06}{12}\right)^{50 \times 12} - 1}{\dfrac{0.06}{12}}$$

$$FV = 100 \times \frac{(1 + 0.005)^{50 \times 12} - 1}{0.005}$$

$$FV = 100 \times \frac{(1.005)^{50 \times 12} - 1}{0.005}$$

The velocity of money

L et's talk about the **velocity** of money. When you save money, you don't really save it. You send it out into the world to zoom around accomplishing stuff and pretending to be a much bigger pile of money than it really is. Surprising? Here's how it works:

Imagine there is a tiny village that is its own country. We'll call it Zurichtensteinburg, and in Z'burg there is a total of $1,000 of printed money. (It's in z-marks, but we'll use conversion to US dollars here.) During the month, these things happen: Greta deposits $300 into her account, and the bank loans Gunter $500. Gunter pays $200 to the electrician for repairs to the lighting in his bookstore. Mathilda, the electrician, buys $325 of supplies and equipment and puts $75 in savings. That means $1,400 worth of money has been spent or saved, even though there is only $1,000 of money to start with. The way money keeps moving is called velocity, and to figure out the number of that measurement, we take:

$$V = \frac{\$1400}{\$1000} = 1.4$$

The resulting 1.4 means the value of all transactions divided by the amount of money in the economy. In the third quarter of 2015, the US economy had a money velocity of 1.35 and annual total transactions (gross domestic product, or GDP) of around $18.6 trillion.

$$FV = 100 \times \frac{19.936 - 1}{0.05}$$

$$FV = 100 \times \frac{18.936}{0.05}$$

$$= 100 \times 3{,}787.1911$$

$$= \$378{,}719.11$$

By comparison, let's say you wait until you're thirty-five and save each month until you are seventy:

$$FV = 100 \times \frac{\left(1 + \frac{0.06}{12}\right)^{35 \times 12} - 1}{\frac{0.06}{12}}$$

$$FV = 100 \times \frac{\left(1 + 0.005\right)^{35 \times 12} - 1}{0.005}$$

$$FV = 100 \times \frac{8.124 - 1}{0.005}$$

$$FV = 100 \times \frac{7.124}{0.005}$$

$$= 100 \times 1{,}424.7103$$

$$= \$142{,}471.03$$

That's $236,248 that just more or less disappeared into thin air. If you ever wanted a super power, then being able to make money from being smart about the numbers is it. You can use that money to support a lot of people and projects doing good in the world or to take care of your family while *you* go and do the good deeds.

Grandparents are always saying stuff like, "When I was a boy, you could buy a whole car for $1.75," or "In my day, $10 was a good allowance!" Well, I'm sorry to say, you will likely be saying that, too. The fact is, over time, the value of a dollar keeps going down. This is known as inflation—it costs more money to buy the same item now than it did years ago. We can represent this as a kind of interest formula, but this time the value is going down instead of up:

$$A = P(1 + i)^n$$

where:

A = Amount after n years.
P = Original amount.
i = Rate of inflation.

Using current rates, average decline is around 3 percent, so let's plug in $100 as a starting value. We find that in twenty years:

$$A = \$100 \times (1 - 0.03)^{20} = \$100 \times 0.54379 = \$54.38$$

That means if you spend $100 at the grocery store twenty years from now, you will only get about the amount of stuff you could buy now for $54.

Credit card crunch

Time after time, when people sit down and look at the real math behind using those oh-so-easy credit cards, they are shocked.

They realize how much paying by credit card actually ends up costing them in the end. Let's see what happens in credit card **amortization**. That's when people pay off the money borrowed plus interest in regular, even payments.

If we take out a loan for a given amount of money at a certain interest rate, then we can use the following equation to quickly crunch the numbers to show how much interest we will end up paying in the end.

The formula for the monthly payments is:

$$M = \frac{P}{\dfrac{1 - (1 + i)^{-n}}{i}}$$

where:

M = Monthly payment.
P = Principal (the original amount borrowed).
i = The interest rate per period.
n = The number of periods.

So, for instance, let's say you spent $1,000 on a credit card with an 18 percent annual rate. Let's say you aim to pay it off in 36 months (three years). We divide the 18 percent annual interest rate (0.18) by 12 months to get 0.015, our value for i, the interest rate for one pay period.

$$M = \frac{1000}{\dfrac{1 - (1 + 0.015)^{-n}}{0.015}}$$

Plug in 36 months as *n*:

$$M = \frac{1000}{\frac{1 - (1 + 0.015)^{-36}}{0.015}}$$

$$M = \frac{1000}{\frac{1 - 0.5851}{0.015}}$$

$$M = \frac{1000}{\frac{0.41491}{0.015}}$$

$$M = \frac{1000}{27.66}$$

$$M = \$36.15 \text{ per month}$$

That total is slightly higher than the minimum payment your credit card company will probably offer (which would take longer to pay off). Now let's plug in the formula that will show how much interest you paid in total for that credit card loan of $1,000:

$$I = nM - P$$
$$I = 36 \times \$36.15 - \$1,000$$
$$I = \$300$$

Even though you only borrowed $1,000, you wound up paying $1,300 back! Now, let's be clear: amortization is not what makes credit cards so easy to misuse. We use amortization for things like paying off student loans and buying a house, too. What makes it easy to overextend on credit cards is the high, high interest rate that we have to pay over the course of the amortization.

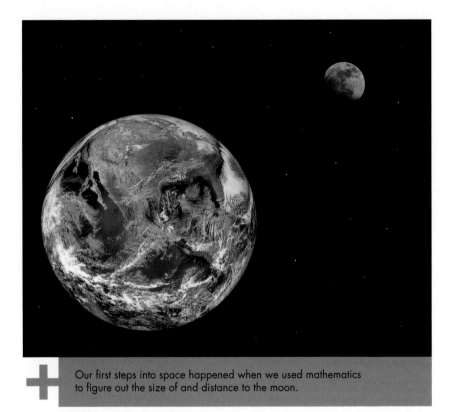

Our first steps into space happened when we used mathematics to figure out the size of and distance to the moon.

Our Pale Blue Dot

The famous astronomer Carl Sagan helped give us some perspective by pointing out that as large as our world and affairs seem to us, when looked at from the bigger view of space, we're really just a pale blue dot.

A Sieve for Primes

Eratosthenes of Cyrene was born around 276 BCE, in Cyrene, Libya, and he died in 194 BCE. He was a Leonardo da Vinci type of figure, widely known for being incredibly good at a wide range of pursuits—including history, poetry, mathematics, science, grammar, and even some philosophy.

Most know him for his work as an astronomer who came up with a measurement for the size of the Earth. But he also devised the clever procedure for finding all the prime numbers—it is called the Sieve of Eratosthenes. It is still widely considered the simplest method for identifying the early primes, and it is much faster than testing the divisibility of different numbers.

The method is to write all the numbers out on a chart in order. Then starting from 2 and moving upward, mark out that number. Then mark out each of its multiples moving along the chart. So, for instance, when you determine that 7 is prime, you would mark it out (or color in its square, or whatever) and then go ahead and mark 14, 21, 35, and on.

In addition to accomplishments in various fields, he was also the librarian for the fabled Library at Alexandria in Egypt.

I have always found that to be an entertaining **paradox** because the first steps we took in reaching out with our scientific minds to understand space were done by using this little blue ball as a measuring stick. I also find it entertaining that we take for granted certain things like how big or how far away the moon and sun are, how big around the Earth is, and so on. And yet, if most people were whisked away to the time of the ancient Greeks, they couldn't explain how we figured out such common elements of our worldview. Could you? How would you figure out how big the moon is? How would you start to puzzle out our distance to the sun?

Well, let's walk through a few of these foundational things. We'll see if that doesn't just make us feel a little smarter than we did when we rolled out of bed this morning.

Let's start with figuring out, even within a reasonable distance, the circumference of the Earth. Would it surprise you if I said it was a Greek mathematician who figured out a way to do it? His name was Eratosthenes, and he was puzzling over the question when he came up with the following approach. He compared the angle of the sunlight in two different cities at the same time. In one city the sun was shining straight down a well, but at a city 500 miles (805 km) away, the rays of the sun were hitting at an angle of 7.2 degrees.

He reasoned that if 7.2 degrees was the effect of 500 miles, then 360 degrees around the whole Earth must mean that:

$$\frac{7.2°}{360°} = \frac{500 \text{ mi}}{\text{Total circumference}}$$

The result was 25,000 miles (40,234 km). He was only off by about 100 miles (160 km)! Of course, the Greeks knew a lot about pi, so once he had this estimate for the circumference, it was a short step to come up with an estimate for the radius of the Earth as well.

OK, I'll admit, the math wasn't exactly amazing by itself, but that's just getting warmed up. Besides, before you dismiss it so quickly, allow that as simple as it might seem to you now, a few minutes ago you were in no better position to solve the puzzle than all the brilliant men and women born before Eratosthenes came along.

So, how could we figure out how far away the moon is without any way of traveling there? As shown in the diagram, we take two cities that are 6,155 miles (9,905 km) apart. When the moon appears directly over one city, it will look like it is just on the horizon to those looking from the other city.

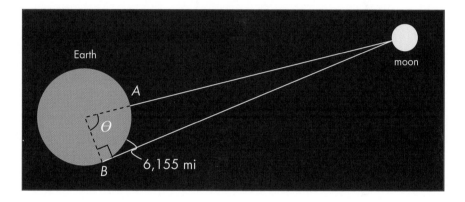

So angle θ must fit the following proportion:

$$\frac{\theta}{360} = \frac{6,155}{24,900}$$

θ comes out to be 88.98°.

We can plug in that the **hypotenuse** = $\dfrac{b}{\cos(88.98°)}$

The radius of the Earth is 3,960 miles (6,373 km), which is b. So the distance to the moon is:

$$a = \frac{3960}{\cos(88.98°)}$$

$$a = \frac{3960}{0.017801}$$

$$a = 222{,}454 \text{ miles}$$

Once again, this is only a ballpark estimate, and we now know using modern technology that the distance to the moon is about 240,000 miles (386,243 km).

In perfect fashion, however, these little balls of water and rock hurtling through vast space, as they spin in circles around each other, generate any number of fascinating little cycles that can be modeled with handy-dandy trigonometric functions.

One of these is, naturally enough, the cycle of day and night. While the amplitude of the waves varies depending on **latitude**, a general form of a sinusoidal equation is:

$$y = a \times \sin[\omega(t - c)] + b$$

Consider a far northern location where the longest day of the year is 18.5 hours, the overall average is 12 hours, and the shortest day of the year has only 5.5 hours of sunlight. We could calculate a, the amplitude (or height) of the sine wave, by considering how far apart the longest and shortest days are.

$$a = ½ \times (18.5 - 5.5) = 6.5$$

Since there are 365 days in a year, we know the period for the function to repeat is 365. Sine waves repeat over a period of 2π, so we need to scale the function appropriately:

$$\omega = \frac{2\pi}{360} \approx 0.0172$$

The average daylight of 12 hours results in a shift upward to the curve, so $b = 12$. The "average" days of daylight occur on equinoxes—the first days of spring and fall. Since the first day of spring typically falls on March 21, that means the sine curve has to be bumped to the right by 80 (the 80th day of the year). We can plug those in to get:

$$y = 6.5 \times \sin[0.0172 \times (t - 80)] + 12$$

This equation will tell you the number of hours of sunlight for any day of the year, where t is the number of days from January 1.

In addition to this little cycle created by the sun, we can also turn to consider the cycle of the tides created by the gravitational pull of the moon.

In a small coastal town, the tide reaches its high mark of 12 feet at 7:00 a.m. At 1:00 p.m., the tide hits a low of 8 feet. How could we map that to a cosine function to predict and calculate the tides at any point in their 12-hour cycle?

$$y = a \times \cos[\omega(t - c)] + b$$

Since the cosine can vary from 1 to −1, when it is 1, y would equal $a \times 1 + b$. When it is −1, y would equal $a \times -1 + b$, which is $b - a$.

We also know the high and low marks, giving us a set of equations:

$$a + b = 12$$
$$b - a = 8$$

Let's rewrite the second one:

$$b = 8 + a$$

Then substitute that into the first of the two:

$$a + 8 + a = 12$$
$$2a = 4$$
$$a = 2$$
$$\text{So, } b = 8 + 2 = 10$$

We are also told that the cycle is 12 hours, allowing us to set ω as:

$$\frac{2\pi}{12} = \frac{\pi}{6}$$

Therefore, the final equation to measure the height of the tide in feet given an hour of the day t is:

$$y = 2 \times \cos\left[\frac{\pi}{6} \times (t - 7)\right] + 10$$

Finding Our Way Around

Our little planet is hurtling through space, circling our sun. Our sun is slowly spinning about the center of our galaxy. And our days are filled with scurrying and scrambling back and forth all over our planet. As we try to navigate in our bustling about, there are a few cool ways that math comes into play.

For example, normally we can travel in vehicles like cars and stop slowly when we need to. But sometimes unexpected situations make us want to stop much more quickly. There is an equation for how long it takes to stop safely, and it is used by crash scene investigators to help them reconstruct an accident.

$$D = \frac{1.05(V_1{}^2 - V_2{}^2)}{64.4(K_1 + K_2 + \sin\theta)}$$

where:

D = Braking distance needed (in feet).
V_1 = Initial speed (in feet per second).
V_2 = Desired new, much-lower speed (in feet per second).
K_1 = A constant based on the brakes and tires.
K_2 = A constant based on this particular car's resistance to rolling.
θ = The grade of the highway.

So, for example, if there was a sudden burst of motivation for changing from 55 miles per hour to 30 miles per hour while coming down a road with a slight grade (−2 degrees), how many feet would it take to happen? Let K_1 = 0.4 and K_2 = 0.02.

First convert velocities from miles per hour to feet per second:

$$V_1 = \frac{55 \text{ mi}}{\text{hour}} \times \frac{5280 \text{ ft}}{\text{mile}} \times \frac{1 \text{ hr}}{60 \text{ min}} \times \frac{1 \text{ min}}{60 \text{ sec}} = 80.67 \text{ ft/sec}$$

$$V_2 = \frac{30 \text{ mi}}{\text{hour}} \times \frac{5280 \text{ ft}}{\text{mile}} \times \frac{1 \text{ hr}}{60 \text{ min}} \times \frac{1 \text{ min}}{60 \text{ sec}} = 44.0 \text{ ft/sec}$$

Then put them into main equation:

$$D = \frac{1.05 \times (80.67^2 - 44^2)}{64.4(0.4 + 0.02 + 0.0349)}$$

$$D = \frac{1.05 \times 4,571.65}{64.4 \times 0.3851}$$

$$D = \frac{4,800.23}{24.80} = 193.55 \text{ ft}$$

Suppose, however, it's a case of a lost hiker in the wilderness. There are two ranger stations 100 miles apart along a straight line. The stations pick up the hiker's distress signal at N 42° E bearing from Station A, as shown, and at N 15° W from Station B. How far is the stranded hiker from Station B?

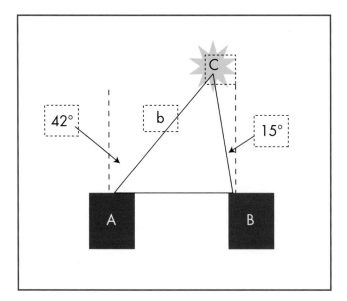

Angle BAC = 90 − 42 = 48°
Angle ABC = 90 − 15 = 75°
Angle ACB = 180 − (48 + 75) = 57°

Now we use the law of sines to find side *b*:

$$\frac{b}{\sin B} = \frac{c}{\sin C}$$

$$\frac{b}{\sin 75°} = \frac{100}{\sin 57°}$$

$$b = \frac{100 \times \sin 75°}{\sin 57°}$$

$$b = 115.17 \text{ miles}$$

Knowing the distance and the bearing will help find the lost hiker. In this case, trigonometry can help save lives.

Alright, good job! Hopefully you came through this chapter at a nice, slow pace. There's no surprise ending where we find out where *x* went and *y* she left (ha!). There are, though, a bunch of mysteries that we solved—from the way blood and impulses travel through our bodies to the moon and Earth zipping through the universe.

In the next chapter, we'll turn to look at some of the ways similar equations and formulas and repeating patterns help people carry out their jobs. This type of math helps people find shortcuts. Remember, the shortcut may not be as short as you want, but it's way shorter than going the long way around!

Every decision a photographer makes changes the elements of an equation for how a picture will turn out.

THREE

Functions in Others' Everyday Lives

A fter looking at the various and interesting ways that functions allow us to make sense of so many things about the world, it should not be surprising to see how much of a role they play in various and interesting careers from taking pictures of fashion models to taking pictures of distant stars and galaxies.

Photographer

There are a number of different kinds of specialists within the field of photography. They might focus on a certain subject, like wildlife or fashion. They also work in different industries, like shooting images for technical manuals or news journalism. Some of the typical skills that would carry over to a lot of the different job types in the group include deciding how to compose the shots, how to improve the image with natural or artificial lighting, and how to develop pictures with chemicals or computer software. They also need many key skills involved in running and managing a business—especially for some of the areas we think of first, like wedding and portrait photographers who are often self-employed.

Focusing distance

Let's start with a fairly simple example of numbers being involved in good photography, and that is adjusting the focus. If the distance between the object and the front of camera lens is reduced, then the distance from the back of the lens to the film surface (or digital optics sensor) has to be increased. Different lenses have different focal lengths. Let's look at the case of a lens with focal length of 50 millimeters:

$$\frac{1}{x} + \frac{1}{y} = \frac{1}{F}$$

where:

x = Distance from object to front edge of lens.
y = Distance from back edge of lens to image surface.
F = Focal length.

So, let's imagine an object 1 meter away ($x = 1000$ mm):

$$\frac{1}{1000} + \frac{1}{y} = \frac{1}{50}$$

Now, solve for y:

$$\frac{1}{y} = \frac{1}{50} - \frac{1}{1000}$$

$$\frac{1}{y} = \frac{1000}{50,000} - \frac{50}{50,000}$$

$$\frac{1}{y} = \frac{950}{50,000} = 52.6 \text{ mm}$$

This means the lens would have to be adjusted 2.6 millimeters away from the image surface to properly focus the photograph.

Viewing angle

Interestingly enough, changing the focal length of the camera lens will also cause a change in the viewing angle. A wide-angle lens will often have a focal length like 28 millimeters. This compares to a telephoto lens, which might have a focal length of 300 millimeters but takes in much less width in the photo. A general formula is:

$$\theta = 2 \times \tan^{-1} \frac{21.634}{x}$$

where:

x = Focal length of lens.
θ = Width of viewing angle.
$\tan^{-1}$ = The inverse function of the tangent, also known as the arctangent.

So let's do the math to see what the difference in viewing angles on those two would be.

For a 300-millimeter telephoto lens:

$$\theta = 2 \times \tan^{-1} \frac{21.634}{x}$$

$$\theta = 2 \times \tan^{-1} \frac{21.634}{300}$$

$$\theta = 2 \times \tan^{-1} 0.07211$$

$$\theta = 2 \times 4.124 = 8.25°$$

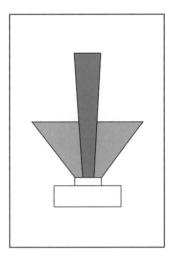

What about for the 28-millimeter wide-angle lens?

$$\theta = 2 \times \tan^{-1} \frac{21.634}{x}$$

$$\theta = 2 \times \tan^{-1} \frac{21.634}{28}$$

$$\theta = 2 \times \tan^{-1} 0.077264$$

$$\theta = 2 \times 37.691 = 75.38°$$

The wide-angle lens can't capture distant subjects, but it shows a much wider view of the area photographed.

Chemical bath and rinse

We have to keep in mind that the thinking and complex problem solving aren't all finished up once the shutter clicks. There are still a lot of decisions that have to be made before a final set of quality photos come out communicating exactly what the photographer and the model wanted to accomplish. A good example of that involves understanding some of the processes that go into developing prints.

One of the final steps in processing black-and-white images is to dunk the print in a chemical solution to seal and stabilize the image. It is then rinsed with water to clear off the excess chemical fixer. Knowing how long you need to rinse the images, though, can prevent a rush job that would end up hurting the quality of the picture. If we know that about 80 percent of the chemicals are cleared away after four minutes of washing, how much chemical residue would probably be left after twenty minutes under the running water?

Well, we know that the rate of rinsing looks like this:

$$A_c = 0.20^n$$

where:

n = Each stretch of 4 minutes.

We can quickly see with a little mental math that if n is 1, the result would be 0.20, which means 20 percent remains and 80 percent is gone—just as we wanted. To find what happens at the end of 5 periods, then, we just need to set n to 5. Remember, that means a total of 20 minutes.

$$A_c = 0.20^5$$

$$A_c = 0.00032, \text{ or } 0.032 \text{ percent}$$

That's a low chemical level that will usually prevent lingering trace amounts from visibly affecting the picture.

Medical Research Scientist

Medical research scientists work to understand the human body in all its complexity in order to find ways to maintain, recover, and extend healthy lives. Their job uses a number of different sciences, from biochemistry to nuclear physics, in order to test out different possible medications, machines, tools, and medical practices. They also spend a large amount of time staying up to date on the research and developments being made by other medical scientists around the world. They share the results of their own research at conferences and through published studies.

Virus

Different viruses will behave in distinctive ways, so with each variant and each new virus, researchers have to figure out its characteristics. A critical trait is the pattern and speed at which the virus spreads among carriers. A representative example for such a calculation is:

$$V_t = \frac{10,000}{5 + 1245e^{-0.97t}}$$

where:

V_t = Number of carriers of the virus.
t = Number of days.

What does that tell us about the number of carriers at day zero?

$$V_t = \frac{10,000}{5 + 1245e^{-0.97 \times 0}}$$

The exponent of 0 on the e means the same as any x^0:

$$V_t = \frac{10,000}{5 + 1245}$$

$$V_t = \frac{10,000}{1250} = 8$$

So eight people were the initial carriers once the virus started to spread.

The next questions have to do with speed and scale. How many carriers will there be by day three if the research team doesn't stop it? How many at day five?

$$V_t = \frac{10,000}{5 + 1245e^{-0.97 \times 3}}$$

$-0.97 \times 3 = -2.9$, so:

$$V_t = \frac{10,000}{5 + 1245e^{-2.9}}$$

Then take e to the power of -2.9:

$$V_t = \frac{10,000}{5 + (1245 \times 0.05502)}$$

Meet Lincoln James

Please meet Lincoln James, a professional photographer, who has agreed to chat with us about how math figures into his career.

Thank you for taking some time out of you schedule to share a few thoughts, Lincoln. Can you tell us what kind of photography you do?

Sure. I guess I'm the kind of photographer most people probably think of when they hear the word. My focus is on working with models and actors and actresses to help them build their portfolios.

What are some different ways and kinds of math that you use in your job?

The most basic understanding is knowing the relationship between the variables in a photograph. Setting the camera speed at 2 seconds will allow a lot of light in, but it means that blurring will happen. Switching the camera to 1/300th of a second means that less light will be let in, so the image will be crisp, but dark. It's always a concession.

To complicate things further, photographers can alter the light sensitivity of the sensors—the ISO range. Higher ISO means less light is needed, but it degrades the image in terms of graininess. The job of the photographer lies in balancing these various factors, knowing how they relate to each other.

Once I've got a model in front of me, it gets even more fun. If I can't keep the variables clear, or get confused in the middle of a shoot as to how all these variables react, the images might end up really dark, really blurred, or really scratchy and grainy. If this happens, the model will hate the images and will not hire me again or recommend me to other people.

Photographers that develop their images in a darkroom with chemicals really need to get the ratios of chemicals right. If you get it wrong? Well, **toxic** clouds of smoke aren't great for your hair. Or your skin. Or breathing, really. Know your math so you can know your proportions!

Is there a kind of math you wish you were better at?

That thing that lets you work out $(4x + 2)$ times $(2x - 3)$ in an instant, or something. It seems like it would help when I'm trying to balance trade-offs between options. It's beyond me, so **quadratic** equations and I don't get along!

$$V_t = \frac{10{,}000}{5 + 68.50391}$$

$$V_t = \frac{10{,}000}{73.5039} = 136.05$$

We round to 136 (because we know 0.05 don't have the disease). Now let's see day five:

$$V_t = \frac{10{,}000}{5 + 1245e^{-0.97 \times 5}}$$

$-0.97 \times 5 = -4.85$, so:

$$V_t = \frac{10{,}000}{5 + 1245e^{-4.85}}$$

Then we calculate e to the power of -4.85:

$$V_t = \frac{10{,}000}{5 + (1245 \times 0.00783)}$$

$$V_t = \frac{10{,}000}{5 + 9.748}$$

$$V_t = \frac{10{,}000}{14.748} = 678.06$$

So 678 people are infected.

There's something cool about this virus, though. OK, not cool in that it's still running wild and making people sick, but mathematically cool. Because any researcher worth keeping alive for more of the movie would check further out than just five days. We could plug this into our computer and find that by day ten, the rate of increase has slowed.

Between days five and six, it goes up 70 percent, but between days ten and eleven, it only goes up 0.9 percent. Always be willing to check numbers further out when making a prediction.

Radioactive isotopes

When researchers study and test certain chemicals for use in medical procedures, they have to provide some very careful and very well-tested numbers. An example of this is when doctors inject **radioactive** iodine into a patient's system in order to help **diagnose** a disorder involving the thyroid. Radioactive means bad, right? Yes, although in some cases, in small doses, it is a small bad in comparison to the larger, more harmful thing we're using it to find and fix. The equation that shows the researchers how much of this toxic substance is still in the patient's system is given by:

$$I_t = 6e^{-0.087t}$$

where:

I_t = Mass of **isotope** remaining in millicuries (mCi).
t = Number of days.

We can plug in and see how much is in the system after one day.

$$I_t = 6e^{-0.087 \times 1}$$
$$I_t = 6 \times 0.91668$$
$$I_t = 5.5 \text{ mCi}$$

Now, remember what we were reminded about a few minutes ago? We should check a number slightly farther out, like ten thousand days! No, just kidding. We would only pick a number way out if we had some reason to think it was worth checking. Let's see how ten days out looks:

$$I_t = 6e^{-0.087 \times 10}$$

$$I_t = 6 \times 0.41895$$

$$I_t = 2.5 \text{ mCi}$$

OK, it's going down pretty quickly. Should the government grant the doctors clearance to start using this radioactive substance on people? I think it would be good to be able to show the government how many days it would take to get the end result down to zero, don't you? Wouldn't you kind of want to see that before they put the radioactive stuff into you?

$$I_t = 6e^{-0.087t}$$

Now we set it to 0 and solve for t:

$$0 = 6e^{-0.087t}$$

Well, for $x \times y$ to equal 0, one of them has to be 0. We can't say $6 = 0$, so let's try setting the e part to 0:

$$0 = e^{-0.087t}$$

You might not remember, but a negative in front of an exponent just means we need to flip it upside down so this part is in the denominator of the fraction:

$$0 = \frac{1}{e^{0.087t}}$$

Now we just have to think about when $\frac{1}{x}$ can equal 0. Hmm ... right, we can't. So, what happens? Well, even though we can't get to 0, think about what size the result would be after one hundred days:

$$I_t = 6e^{-0.087 \times 100}$$

$$I_t = 6e^{-8.7}$$

$$I_t = 6 \times 0.00017 = 0.00102 \text{ mCi}$$

That's a long way from 5.5 and 2.5, right? At one thousand days out, the trace amounts are going to be even tinier.

Medications

Sometimes doctors need to understand how quickly a harmful chemical can go out of the body. In other cases, logically enough, the goal is to figure out how to keep certain levels of helpful chemicals *in* the body. For maintenance medications (medications people need to take as a routine, not just occasionally), researchers need to have a clear idea of what the **cumulative** effect of repeatedly taking meds will do to the levels in a person's system.

Suppose a patient takes a 2-milligram medication every day. During each twenty-four-hour cycle, her body is able to use 40 percent of what is in her system after she takes her morning pills. One of the first questions that researchers need to be able to address is: How much of the chemical would be stored in her body after taking it every day for n days?

The formula for finding how much the meds add up to over time is:

$$\sum_{i=1}^{n} 2 \times (0.6)^i$$

That just shows that we are interested in the sum of days from day 1 to day n. Each day is counted as a separate i. The patient is getting 2 milligrams each day, and 60 percent of it is being stored in her body each day.

To solve that, we *could* calculate each day out by hand. That would be fine if it were two or three days, but it would be very time consuming if we were interested in, say, thirty days' worth of impact. In order to give us a handy-dandy shortcut (our favorite!), we can use this:

$$S = \frac{a_1}{1 - r}$$

where:

S = The sum from an infinite number of days.
a_1 = The amount given each day.
r = The rate it is accumulating.

$$S = \frac{2}{1 - 0.6} = \frac{2}{0.4} = 5 \text{ milligrams}$$

That means she has a cumulative total of 5 milligrams in her system even if she took the medication every day from now until the day the sun goes giant and swallows the Earth (about 7.6 billion years from now). In fact, her system stabilizes at 5 milligrams after only thirty days. But how much of the drug is getting absorbed every day? It should be 2 milligrams × 0.4, or 0.8 milligrams, right? Who's with me?

No. You know better than to go along with me just because it's quicker and easier. She has 5 milligrams in her system after taking morning meds, and her body uses 40 percent of "what's in her system" over the course of the day. Her body uses 5 milligrams × 0.4, or 2 milligrams. She then replaces that 2 milligrams by taking another pill the following morning.

Of course, the first time the researchers set this equation up, they're probably working backwards to find out what the dosage (a_1) should be in the first place in order to create a certain level in the system.

Some careers involve running different mathematical models on different computers at the same time to keep track of all the variables.

Financial Analyst

"Financial analyst" is a very broad category that covers different kinds of jobs. Sometimes a job at one company will have this title, and the exact same job at another company will have a totally different title—like "stock analyst" or "investment analyst." At the heart of it, the role involves using a variety of mathematical tools to figure out what different things are actually worth and what they are going to be worth in the future—both short term and long term. Some of the things that are part of the job in order to help analysts form accurate conclusions and recommendations are: studying trends in business and economics, researching financial information about various companies, and analyzing current and past prices and values.

Should I buy this stock?

One of the import roles financial analysts play involves figuring out how much we should be willing to spend today in order to receive a certain amount of money at some point in the future. Just think about it in simple terms: if you could put your money in two different banks that are otherwise equal, you would put it in the one that gives the largest interest rate, right? They're telling you how much your money will be worth next year, but in exchange for making sure you get that amount, it's pretty low—so they can safely pay you that much. What if they didn't tell you how much money they would be able to pay you next year? Or if they both said, "We'll pay you between 3 percent and 6 percent"? That's a pretty wide range, and most of us would way rather have the doubled amount, so we'd research carefully to see which bank was most likely to be successful next year.

In the case of companies, that's how stocks work. There's not a guarantee how much your little slice of the company will be worth next year. You're willing to take the risk that it will be at least as good as the amount the bank was willing to pay you to let them use your money for a year instead of using it to buy stocks. One of the equations that analysts use to figure out how much you could pay now is called the net present value calculation:

$$V_p = D\,(1 + g) \times \frac{x^n - 1}{g - r}$$

$$\text{and } x = \frac{1 + g}{1 + r}$$

where:

V_p = Present value.
D = **Dividend** (stocks are ownership in the company, so they
  pay stockholders some of the profits).
n = Time in years.
g = The expected growth rate of the dividend.
r = The discount rate, which reflects how risky the stock is.

Let's see an example of how that would play out if the expected
growth rate was 10 percent and the discount rate was 8 percent:

$$x = \frac{1 + 0.10}{1 + 0.08} = \frac{1.10}{1.08} = 1.02$$

Then we plug that into the bigger equation. This year's dividend
was $5 per share of stock:

$$V_p = D(1 + g) \times \frac{x^n - 1}{g - r}$$

$$V_p = 5(1 + 0.10) \times \frac{1.02^1 - 1}{0.10 - 0.08}$$

$$V_p = 5(1 + 0.10) \times \frac{0.02}{0.02}$$

$$V_p = 5 \times 1.10 \times 1 = \$5.50$$

This means that if the stock is currently for sale at a price below
$5.50 per share, it would be a good investment.

How long will it last?

A different kind of problem comes up when we are trying to evaluate how long something will last if it is of a limited supply. Maybe it's the money in our savings account when we retire. Maybe it's the available coal in the United States. (As long as a company stays in business, the shares of stock don't get "used up," so the model is different.) Here's how the formula works:

$$n = \frac{\ln\left(1 + \frac{S}{U}r\right)}{\ln(1 + r)}$$

OK, it looks scary. We've talked about this, though, right? Just untangle it one little piece at a time—like a plate full of spaghetti. I'm betting that tangle never slowed you down.

In this formula:

n = The number of years it will last.
S = The supply.
U = The usage.
r = The rate of additional usage.

To see what this looks like, let's consider a case where a country has a coal reserve that would last for 200 years if their rate of consumption stayed constant. However, if their use of coal continues to go up by 2.1 percent each year (maybe their population is growing; maybe they're becoming more industrialized), the change would look more like this:

$$n = \frac{\ln(1 + 200 \times 0.021)}{\ln(1 + 0.021)}$$

$$n = \frac{\ln 5.2}{\ln 1.021} = \frac{1.64866}{0.02078} = 79.33 \text{ years}$$

That's a far cry from the 200 years we were talking about a minute ago. Let's contrast that, though, and see what happens instead if a country is able to cut that rate in half: down to 1.05 percent each year compared to 2.1 percent. In that situation, take a second to predict what you think would happen. Will it be halfway between 200 and 79.33? Let's see:

$$n = \frac{\ln(1 + 200 \times 0.0105)}{\ln(1 + 0.0105)}$$

$$n = \frac{\ln 3.1}{\ln 1.0105} = \frac{1.1314}{0.01045} = 108.26 \text{ years}$$

Compare that to the prediction you might have found appealing:

$$79.33 + \frac{200 - 79.33}{2} = 139.67 \text{ years}$$

The gap has to do with the effect of the compounding, so it doesn't work quite like our intuition might tempt us to think.

Animated Film Director

The film director is really the one who owns the vision for bringing a story to life for the audience. While they may have staff and other specialists helping them, depending on the size of the production and the nature of the film, directors are the key decision makers on nearly every aspect of a project, from selecting cast members and editing the script to the choices of costuming, set design, lighting, soundtrack, and so on. They are the ones who imagine the story in their mind, building on what the author has said. Then they try to work with others to bring their imagined version to life for everyone else to see. In order to do this well, they need to know something about all the different jobs that go into the creation. They manage the process, from coaching the actors to collaborating with investors and the business team who will help finance and market the film.

Making waves

There are a variety of techniques which are all combined together to try to simulate real waves, and there are some much more advanced mathematical theories that attempt to get it perfectly. Looking at a couple of basic examples here should give you a good sense of how the same math we've been talking about would be involved.

Here we see an example where a periodic wave form is being shifted to the right, creating the illusion of movement. If you think for a minute, each water wave itself doesn't go up and down like it's a bobbing cork, right? It moves more like the water has popped a wheelie on its bike and is pedaling forward.

To animate this, the computer program would be slowly advancing the number t, for the time value, and the curve would slowly be moving across.

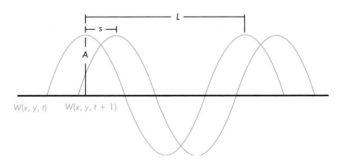

Here:

L = Wavelength: the crest-to-crest distance between waves.
A = Amplitude: the height of the wave from the water axis to
the wave crest.
s = Speed: the distance the curve moves per second.

The waves are then given a direction of movement. In the image on page 94, it is straight across from left to right. But the movement could be in any direction.

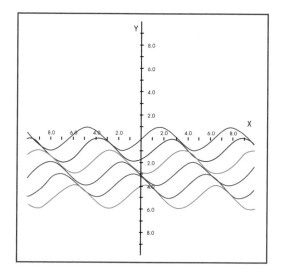

Once a bunch of these waves are mapped onto the images of the film animation sequence, a moving surface is created, instead of the appearance of a whole bunch of separate math diagrams.

A somewhat more complex kind of movement is created by adding another direction. Instead of having the curves move in that direction in a straight line, they move up and down along an additional curve. Then programmers start adding in how waves shift when they bump into each other, how they dampen (they become less and less tall), and so on.

Meet Eric Anderson

Please meet Eric Anderson, a producer and director perhaps best known for the award-winning animated short film *The Looking Planet*. With a degree in English and an MFA in film and computer animation, he has been a director for thirteen years.

It's amazing to see the list of awards for The Looking Planet. *I think that probably deserves a whole book of its own. Perhaps for now you could talk to us about what in the world math has to do with something like being an award-winning movie director.*

Basic arithmetic is in everything. Lots of frame counting. There are twenty-four frames per second in film and its digital counterpart. So I'm constantly keeping track of numbers in my head to know how long a shot or a sequence is. With computer animation especially, the whole world inside the computer is a computational construct. And even though in many cases the software makes it possible to do things like calculate light rays, gravity, wind, and vortex forces without having to do anything other than set parameters, you still need to have a good grasp on what the computer is doing. If you have complex shots, sometimes you have to dig in and do some algebra and calculus to get the computer animation to behave the way you want it to.

Can you give us an example?

For instance, to get a believable water simulation, there is a lot of math happening, especially for something as seemingly simple as a small creature coming out of the water. It quickly gets to a level where you have to put in your own formulas for the particle simulation to behave in a predictable manner that fits with what you need for a shot.

Is there a kind of math or kind of math problem you wish you were better at?

I wish I had been better at algebra and calculus because these computational tools come up all the time in computer animation. Just working with basic variables is so important to how the computer generates complex imagery. I have to rely on others who understand it better than I, and that's frustrating for me. I wish I had more mastery so that I better reach what I am after as a director.

Astronomer

The career of an astronomer involves the scientific investigation of outer space and everything in it. They form hypotheses, conduct experimental tests, collect and analyze data, and work to build and test complex models. They hope to understand space objects like planets, stars, and galaxies. They also examine the forces at work, like the nature of gravity. Their work involves the use of sophisticated computer systems, advanced telescopes, and high-tech materials. It also involves a lot of work sharing their research and writing for grants, as well as reading and discussing the research of other astronomers.

Star light, star bright

One of the key pieces of information that lays the groundwork for further research on a star is to calculate the perceived brightness of a star to the human eye. That's called a star's **magnitude**, and its equation is:

$$M = -2.5 \times \log\left(\frac{B}{B_0}\right)$$

where:

M = Magnitude.
B = The actual brightness of the star.
B_0 = A constant that is based on the dimmest stars that are visible to the naked eye.

$$M = -2.5 \times \log\left(\frac{B}{B_0}\right)$$

First, we're going to unpack the right side using log rules:

$$M = -2.5 \times \log B + 2.5 \times \log B_0$$

Interestingly enough, the brighter a star is, the lower its magnitude. That seems opposite from what you would expect, but let's run a simple example to illustrate. We know that Star 1 is brighter than Star 2 by approximately 100 times. Here, the subscript 1 stands for Star 1, and the same goes for 2.

$$M_1 = -2.5 \times \log B_1 + 2.5 \times \log B_0$$
$$M_2 = -2.5 \times \log B_2 + 2.5 \times \log B_0$$

Since Star 1 is 100 times brighter than Star 2, we can substitute:

$$M_1 = -2.5 \times \log(100B_2) + 2.5 \times \log B_0$$

Using our rules again, we can split the terms:

$$M_1 = -2.5 \times \log 100 - 2.5 \times \log B_2 + 2.5 \times \log B_0$$
$$M_1 = -2.5 \times \log 100 + (-2.5 \times \log B_2 + 2.5 \times \log B_0)$$

Notice how the last part is the same as M_2 above.

$$M_1 = -2.5 \times \log 100 + M_2$$
$$M_1 = -2.5 \times 2 + M_2$$
$$M_1 = -5 + M_2$$

This means the magnitude of the first, brighter star is five less than the second star. There are some different versions of the equation that get used. In this case, the constant of B_0 would already have been adjusted to account for some of those alternative versions.

Some stars don't just twinkle when the light comes through the atmosphere. A variable star changes its brightness like someone moving a dimmer switch.

Stars with mood swings

Some stars are characterized by the fact that their brightness varies in a repeating cycle, or period. Astronomers call those stars variable stars. Here is how the brightness can change for one of many possible examples of these stars:

$$B_t = 7.8 - 2.2 \times \cos\left(\frac{\pi t}{150}\right)$$

where:

B = Brightness.
t = Days.

This equation allows us to calculate the period—the number of days until the pattern repeats. Since the cosine function repeats every 2π, we can just divide by the term inside the cosine part of the formula:

$$\frac{2\pi}{\frac{\pi}{150}} = 2 \times 150 = 300 \text{ days}$$

We can also evaluate the minimum and maximum brightness in a similar fashion as we have seen with other functions. Here we know that cosine varies between 1 and −1, so the two extremes of the wave are:

$$7.8 - 2.2 \times 1 = 5.6$$
$$7.8 - 2.2 \times -1 = 10$$

Hmm ... I feel like my brightness goes up and down some days, too. I wonder if that means I have a variable magnitude.

Fasten your seatbelts

I mentioned earlier in the book that our planet is our pale blue dot hurtling through space, as you might remember. Well, let's take a look at just how fast we're going. We will start with some key things we already know. The radius of our trip around the sun is 93 million miles (150 million km). Although our orbit is not a perfect circle (it's an ellipse, as with other planets), we're close enough to use a circle in this situation.

First we need the circumference of this big trip. We remember that:

$$C = \pi \times \text{diameter}$$
$$C = \pi \times (2 \times 93{,}000{,}000)$$
$$C = 584{,}336{,}230 \text{ miles}$$

Now you might not know this, but our planet's speed is not always exactly the same, since we're not a perfect circle in our orbit.

We speed up a bit more when closer to the sun. But, again, for our purposes, we can pretend we're a nice circle. We take one year to make one complete trip around the sun. To calculate our speed, we just convert the units:

$$S = 584{,}336{,}230 \text{ miles}/365 \text{ days}$$

$$S = 1{,}600{,}921 \text{ miles per day}$$

$$S = \frac{1.6\text{M miles}}{1 \text{ day}} \times \frac{1 \text{ day}}{24 \text{ hours}} = \frac{1.6\text{M miles}}{24 \text{ hours}}$$

$$= 66{,}705 \text{ miles per hour (or } 107{,}351 \text{ kmh)}$$

If you could travel that fast on land, you'd circle the Earth more than two and a half times in an hour!

Meteorite off the starboard bow

Occasionally, with all the pieces of stuff whipping around in space like little kids running around the playground hopped up on sugar from their morning snacks, some of those pieces are going to crash into each other. Sometimes one of those things is a meteorite and sometime the other one is us. In order to know how long we have until some hero flies up there in their super ship to blast the meteorite with lasers (or photon torpedoes, or leftover holiday fruitcake, or whatever), we need the astronomers to figure out how fast it's zooming toward us.

One of the equations involved looks like this:

$$V = \frac{k}{\sqrt{d}}$$

where:

k = A constant.
d = Distance from Earth.
V = Velocity in kilometers per second.

Then set k = 300 and have the meteorite zooming toward us from 25,000 kilometers out:

$$V = \frac{300}{\sqrt{25,000}} = 1.897 \text{ kilometers per second}$$

$$= 1.179 \text{ miles per second}$$

I will leave it to you to crunch the last couple numbers to see how many seconds or minutes we have before the thing crashes into us. It might be about as long as a sci-fi movie about this scenario.

Mercury

Being able to understand the conditions and features on planets that are difficult (or impossible) to observe involves being able draw conclusions based on the information we can see. To understand the climate on another planet, for instance, its closeness to the sun (and how much its closeness changes over the course of a year) is a major factor. Mercury makes its way around the sun in an orbit shaped like an ellipse. The equation is:

$$r = \frac{3.44 \times 10^7}{1 - 0.206 \times \cos \theta}$$

where:

r = Radius (distance to the sun) in miles.
θ = A portion of the orbit, measured in degrees.

Scientists are dividing some temperature data into groups based on distance from the sun. How much of Mercury's orbit is at least 3.09×10^7 miles away from the sun?

We need to find θ. We know the new radius we're looking for:

$$r = \frac{3.44 \times 10^7}{1 - 0.206 \times \cos \theta} = 3.09 \times 10^7$$

Multiply both sides by the denominator:

$$3.44 \times 10^7 = (3.09 \times 10^7)(1 - 0.206 \times \cos \theta)$$

Divide both by 10^7:

$$3.44 = 3.09(1 - 0.206 \times \cos \theta)$$

Distribute the 3.09:

$$3.44 = 3.09 - 0.63654 \times \cos \theta$$
$$3.44 - 3.09 = -0.63654 \times \cos \theta$$

Multiply both sides by −1 to clear out the negative sign on the right:

$$3.09 - 3.44 = 0.63654 \times \cos \theta$$

Divide both sides by 0.63654:

A bright astronomer

Henrietta Swan Leavitt, born July 4, 1868, was an American astronomer. Her discoveries helped open the door for Ejnar Hertzsprung to figure out the distance of stars, Harlow Shapley to calculate the size of the Milky Way, and Edwin Hubble to figure out that the universe is expanding.

Leavitt graduated from Radcliffe College. Then she worked at Harvard University, helping to catalog and classify a large collection of photographic plates from the university's observatory. It was during this work classifying over 1,700 photographic images that she discovered a direct relationship between the apparent brightness of variable stars and their periods. The brighter stars had longer periods.

The logarithm of the star's period lines up with its average brightness. This created a measurement that would allow scientists to analyze galaxies farther than one hundred light years away. (The older **parallax** method is not useful past that limit.) Until this point, there was not an easy way to tell whether a star appeared dim because it was close but dim, or because it was bright but much farther away.

One thing is certain: Leavitt's brightness was off the charts. Hubble, the astronomer credited with figuring out that certain nebulae were actually galaxies outside of our own, said that the Nobel Prize should have gone to Leavitt.

$$(3.09 - 3.44)/0.63654 = \cos \theta$$
$$-0.54985 = \cos \theta$$

Take the arccos (it's the inverse of the cosine):

$$\theta = 123.357 \text{ degrees}$$

So 123 degrees of Mercury's orbit is at least 3.09×10^7 miles away from the sun. Since there are 360 degrees in an orbit, that means about one third (123/360) of the time, Mercury is at that distance or greater.

Look at you! You have planets and numbers all spinning around the sun in your head like Galileo. The celestial objects move in patterns and cycles like a complicated ballroom dance.

Environmental Scientist

This career is focused on applying science skills to study, test, and implement different measures to prevent or correct environmental disruptions. Some of their roles could include supervising the improvement of polluted areas, collaborating with government and industry personnel, and researching the environment. There are also, as you might guess, a large variety of different actual roles that fall under this career heading—from climate change specialists to industrial ecologists.

Ocean salinity

Salinity is the amount of salt dissolved in water. Because so many marine ecosystems depend on a narrow range of salinity levels in a given region, environmental scientists must monitor these carefully while taking into account the natural variations for different latitudes and different ocean depths.

For salinity levels up to 1,000 meters (3,280 feet) below the surface at a given latitude, the following equation is the working model:

The circulation system of ocean currents creates measurable patterns in salt levels, and that allows us to track their "health" like sodium in your bloodstream.

$$S_x = 32.4 + 1.4 \times \log(x + 1)$$

where:

S_x = The salinity level at depth x (grams of salt per kilogram of water).
x = Depth in meters.

So, where would our scientists expect the salinity level to fall for a sample from 500 meters?

$$S_x = 32.4 + 1.4 \times \log(x + 1)$$
$$S_x = 32.4 + 1.4 \times \log(500 + 1)$$
$$S_x = 32.4 + 1.4 \times 2.6998$$
$$S_x = 36.17 \text{ grams per kilogram}$$

Of course, that number by itself doesn't actually tell them anything meaningful until it is placed into context with other numbers. Is this higher than usual? Lower than usual? Is it about the same level as other samples from nearby locations? Has it suddenly changed? Those kinds of questions allow the environmental scientist to give some meaning in terms of explaining or predicting a change.

Air quality

This issue provides a good opportunity to take a deep breath and reflect on something. While we look for patterns and similarities from one math problem or application to the next, we should be careful not to overdo it, anymore than if we were to focus so intently on what birds have in common that we stop noticing the differences in color or song. If we look at a couple examples of functions that allow for the mapping and forecasting of carbon dioxide levels in the atmosphere, we can notice how they also show slight variations.

In one city, the equation that maps air quality data collected is:

$$L_A = 0.022x^2 + 0.55x + 316 + 3.5 \times \sin(2\pi x)$$

where:

L_A = The air pollution, measured in parts per million, in city A.
x = The time in years from a baseline year (for example, number of years since 1970).

In another city, the equation is:

$$L_B = 0.04x^2 + 0.6x + 330 + 7.5 \times \sin(2\pi x)$$

Before we move forward, take a few minutes to look at them and ask yourself which one you think is in a more dire circumstance.

Which of our two cities modeled here will likely have the widest fluctuations from one year to the next?

Then make sure you try to walk through the problem. Which one do you think will likely have the worst air quality in twenty more years? Give yourself reasons.

Water toxicity

Environmental scientists do not just work on large-scale projects like the ocean or the atmosphere; they also deal with local-scale impacts and issues, like monitoring local rivers, lakes, and streams for the presence of harmful changes.

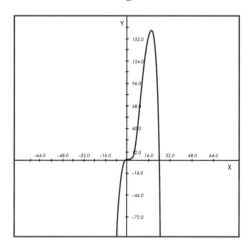

If a researcher is measuring the concentration level of harmful chemicals, there might be an acceptable margin of parts per million that normally enter the river each day from a factory upstream. (It will take more than math to make sense out of why the factory is allowed to dump any parts per million into the river.) An equation like this can help the researcher track to see how that concentrated area of chemicals behaves after it has been in the river a certain amount of time:

$$T_x = -0.005x^4 + 0.12x^3 - 0.04x^2 + 0.015x$$

where:

T_x = Toxin levels.

x = Time in days after chemicals are released into the river.

To appreciate what this shows, seeing the graph on page 109 is really helpful. This graph allows the researcher to see valuable things like the rate the cloud of chemicals travels downstream, times the concentration will be highest (and how high) at this sample location, and so on. Note how the concentration really spikes around sixteen days after the chemicals are released, and then they disappear over the next eight days.

Dark pollution

One of the many ways chemical changes in the water can have a harmful impact on the ecosystems in oceans, lakes, or rivers (and the ecosystems that feed on them) is by changing the amount of light that reaches different underwater levels. If there are elements that cloud the water even small amounts, that keeps the light from traveling as far in the water, and it means that organisms that depend on that light (such as plants) will be affected.

Let's look at the effect of changing the light intensity even small amounts. The general form of the equation for light intensity reaching a given depth of water is:

$$I = I_0 e^{cd}$$

where:

I = Light intensity reaching that depth.
I_0 = The intensity of light at the surface.
c = The measure of cloudiness in the water.
d = The depth being evaluated.

In sample 1, let's set c at -0.002 and test the light intensity at depths of 50 feet and 100 feet:

$$I = I_0 e^{cd}$$

$$I = I_0 e^{-0.002 \times 50}$$

$$= I_0 \times 0.90 = 90 \text{ percent of the starting intensity}$$

$$I = I_0 e^{cd}$$

$$I = I_0 e^{-0.002 \times 100}$$

$$= I_0 \times 0.818 = 82 \text{ percent}$$

In contrast, then, let's see what happens when c goes to -0.003:

$$I = I_0 e^{cd}$$

$$I = I_0 e^{-0.003 \times 50}$$

$$= I_0 \times 0.86 = 86 \text{ percent}$$

$$I = I_0 e^{cd}$$

$$I = I_0 e^{-0.003 \times 100}$$

$$= I_0 \times 0.74 = 74 \text{ percent}$$

Those might not seem like big changes to you. Getting an 86 on a homework assignment, for instance, is not that far from a 90. However, think about it this way: for the critters at 100 feet down, it went from 82 to 74, only 8 percentage points. Dropping 8 percentage points down from 80 is a 10 percent drop, though. If we suddenly cut the amount of food you had to eat tomorrow by 10 percent, would that feel like only a small difference?

Civil Engineer

Civil engineers are the people who plan and build a range of things for the well-being of the city—airports, subway tunnels, bridges, water systems, and more. Some of the things going on for them are very similar across their different specialty areas. They test materials and project sites, maintain and repair current **infrastructure** elements, and design and build scale models. They also prepare and present findings in relation to bid proposals, legal statements, and environmental impact studies.

A gravity grade

In planning the layout of roads and highways through uneven areas, the engineers must take into account the capacities and limitations of the vehicles that will travel the roadway. One part of that puzzle has to do with the grade of the road. Grade is a measure of how steeply the ground is rising. The steeper the grade, the more gravitational force there will be pulling on the vehicle.

$$R_g = W \times \sin \theta$$

where:

R_g = The gravitational resistance at work.
W = The weight of the vehicle.
θ = The angle of the grade. If it's up from horizontal, the slope is positive. If it's down from horizontal, the slope is negative.

Let's look at an example of how that translates into a particular case. Let's say we have a truck and trailer weighing 80,000 pounds traveling up a grade of 5 percent—which means it climbs 5 feet per 100 feet traveled. What would be the effect on the truck?

First we need to calculate sin θ. Imagine a triangle with a base of 100 feet and a height of 5 feet. We need to figure out the hypotenuse. We can use the Pythagorean theorem, and then treat sin θ as the opposite side from the angle (the height) divided by the hypotenuse.

$$h = \sqrt{5^2 + 100^2}$$

$$h = \sqrt{10,025}$$

$$\sin \theta = \frac{5}{\sqrt{10,025}}$$

Now we can plug that into our equation.

$$R_g = 80,000 \times \frac{5}{\sqrt{10,025}}$$

$$= 3,995 \text{ pounds pulling on the truck due to gravity}$$

It might not seem like that big of a deal when thinking just about the weight, but again, if we put this information into a larger context, it takes on some value. For instance, if the number of roads in a given region have a high average for grade (such as roads in the mountains) then it's going to mean increased fuel use, an increase in exhaust **emissions** (because engines have to work harder), and so on. This particular slope will also have a large or small impact on slowing traffic speeds, so depending on the normal traffic flow, there could be an effect like having a clogged artery.

Passing distances

A second, closely related function in planning out road construction in relation to grades is the distances between curves and hills to allow drivers to see oncoming traffic far enough ahead to make smart decisions about passing. These distances depend on the steepness of the road and the speed limit (someone coming over a hill at 30 miles per hour is closing the distance to you more slowly than at 50 miles per hour, so it's *as if* that car is farther away). One possible equation to map passing distance in relation to the speed of a car might be:

$$D_m = -0.002x^3 + 0.442x^2 + 16.42x + 313.5$$

I won't tell you what the variables are this time. Think through for yourself what D_m probably stands for. (As a hint, the *m* stands for "minimal," which means the least amount allowable.) What is *x*? What are the proper units?

Highway curves

One design feature of highways that you have probably noticed (but also probably did not wonder about the math behind) is that when you are going around highway curves, the road itself is tilted so that the outside is higher than the inside of the curve. You can see this more pronounced at most racetracks.

This is done to help make highways safer, as it **counteracts** some of the forces that would normally pull a car to the outside edge and reduce the force holding the car to the road. This is even more pronounced in situations like rain or wind or ice where the friction is lower than normal. In order to calculate how much the outside should be tilted compared to the inside, the engineers factor in both the radius of the curve and the speed at which the car is traveling (or is *supposed* to be traveling) on that highway. The general equation is:

$$R_c = \frac{s^2}{4.5 + 32.2 \times \tan \theta}$$

where:

R_c = The radius of the curve.
s = Speed the vehicle is traveling in feet per second.

If the radius of a given curve is 1,150 feet and the speed limit is 55 miles per hour, what should the elevation of the outside edge be?

$$R_c = \frac{s^2}{4.5 + 32.2 \times \tan \theta}$$

We need to translate speed to feet per second. 55 miles per hour = 80.8 feet per second.

$$1150 = \frac{80.8^2}{4.5 + 32.2 \times \tan \theta}$$

Multiply both sides by the denominator:

$$1150 \times (4.5 + 32.2 \times \tan \theta) = 80.8^2$$

Divide both sides by 1150:

$$(4.5 + 32.2 \times \tan \theta) = \frac{6.528.64}{1150}$$

$$4.5 + 32.2 \times \tan \theta = 5.67708$$

Subtraction time:

$$32.2 \times \tan \theta = 5.67708 - 4.5$$

$$32.2 \times \tan \theta = 1.17708$$

Why does division always split us apart?

$$\tan \theta = \frac{1.17708}{32.2}$$

$$\tan \theta = 0.03656$$

Now for some arctan action to reverse the tangent:

$$\theta = \tan^{-1} 0.03656 = 2.0938 \text{ degrees} = 2.1 \text{ degrees}$$

I don't know about you, but that's kind of cool to see. By way of comparison, the radius (at the four "corners") and edge elevation for the Daytona Speedway, where they have the Daytona 500, are 1,000 feet, and the bank is 31 degrees. Feel free to run the math to see what the speeds on those turns could be!

CONCLUSION

OK. Let's hear it. How did the experiment go? How did you react to all the functions that model our lives? If you were fair and open minded and really tried to pretend it was interesting, then well done! If you didn't, then go back and read the introduction again.

Remember, if you were fair, but still don't find math to have any cool parts or ideas, then no big deal. Some stuff in life we do because it has to get done, and we have to own it and do well and then move past it.

Here's the more important question: Do you feel a little bit smarter than you were when you started the book? Did you go through the examples again when it felt kind of confusing?

Here's the even more important more important question: Did you discover that you have some curiosity or some persistence or some clever thinking that you didn't realize you had? Did you have to stretch a little bit to pretend you were more curious than you thought? Did you pretend you would stick with things longer than you would if you weren't trying to act like this character? (That is a magic trick of epic proportions.)

Those are all things that will make you better at math as you go forward in life. Long after you forget the examples from this book. Long after you forget the name of that awesome woman who made most of modern astronomy possible. Being able to pretend a little bit and have an open mind will help. Realizing that being fast and being good are not the same thing will help you, too. Pretending

If you do a little pretending and then act the part, stories where you are the awesome character can actually come to life.

you are something builds up some of the muscles inside you and makes you better at it.

Now, for those of you who *did* reread any parts where you got stuck, and *did* pretend like a new puzzle was some cool, shiny rock you discovered, or a kind of butterfly you've never seen—you are on the path to greatness. I mean that. Being able and willing to do that will give you an advantage over 80 percent of people you will compete with in the world. Being able to do that about math will give you a competitive advantage over about 90 percent of the people out in the world. Math is a powerful tool—more powerful than war, or the planets, or the temptation for an extra piece of cake on your birthday.

Once you've closed this book and put it back on the shelf, you need to remember: if someone says something is too hard, change that in your head to the experiment version. It might be too hard, which also allows the alternative option some room to be true. That option says, "It *might be* easy, because of my awesomeness and my not-giving-up-ness." Then you get to be the director of your own movie.

Glossary

amortization The repayment of a loan with interest through regular equal payments.

amplitude The maximum extent of a vibration; the farthest distance above and below the initial resting position.

coefficient The number placed as a multiplier in front of some variable, as in $5x$, where 5 is the coefficient of the variable x.

component A part or element of a larger whole.

cosine The trigonometric function representing the ratio of the side adjacent θ to the hypotenuse.

counteract To act in an opposite way or direction from something to reduce its effect.

cumulative Additive; including amounts or elements that came before.

diagnose To identify a problem or illness that is preventing a system from working correctly.

diastolic The lowest part of the blood pressure cycle occurring at the relaxation/expansion of the heart.

displacement The result of moving something away from its initial position.

dividend A portion of profits paid periodically by a company to its stockholders.

emissions The chemical substances given off, or created by, a process.

exponential Growing or increasing in a manner represented by exponents. For example, 2, 4, 8, and 16 are the first four powers of 2^n.

frequency The rate at which something occurs or repeats in a given period of time.

function An equation that assigns one output value (a y) to each input value (an x).

hypotenuse The longest side of a right triangle, opposite the right angle.

infrastructure The basic structures and facilities needed for operation of an organization or government.

inverse The opposite or the reverse of something. In math, it often means the action which undoes an operation, such as multiplying by $1/x$ instead of by x.

isotopes Different forms of the same element. An isotope is determined by an element's number of neutrons. The number of protons is constant for any given element.

latitude An angular measurement of a location north or south of the equator.

magnitude The degree or extent of something in reference to an initial value.

maximum The greatest amount; in mathematical graphs it refers to the point at which the greatest y value is reached.

micrometer A distance equaling 1/1000th of a millimeter.

minimum The smallest or least amount; in mathematical graphs, it refers to the point at which the lowest y value is reached.

paradox A statement or proposition that seems to be self-contradictory yet makes sense.

parallax The phenomenon that occurs when an object appears to be in different locations if viewed from different reference points.

principal The initial sum of money invested or loaned.

proportion A relationship of equality between two ratios.

quadratic A polynomial in which the highest exponent is two.

radioactive Elements that give off radiation in the form of molecule fragments.

salinity The amount of saline (salt) contained in a given volume of water.

sine The trig function representing the ratio of the side of the triangle opposite angle θ to the hypotenuse.

snarkleous I can't believe you looked this up in the glossary.

systolic The highest part of the blood pressure cycle following the contraction of the heart.

toxic Poisonous.

velocity The speed of something in a given direction.

Further Reading

Books

Gowers, Timothy, June Barrow-Green, and Imre Leader, eds. *The Princeton Companion to Mathematics*. Princeton, NJ: Princeton University Press, 2008.

Huettenmueller, Rhonda. *Precalculus Demystified: Hard Stuff Made Easy*. New York: McGraw-Hill Education, 2012.

Jackson, Tom, ed. *Mathematics: An Illustrated History of Numbers*. New York: Shelter Harbor Press, 2012.

Pickover, Clifford A. *The Math Book: From Pythagoras to the 57th Dimension, 250 Milestones in the History of Mathematics*. New York: Sterling, 2009.

Simmons, George F. *Precalculus Mathematics in a Nutshell: Geometry, Algebra, Trigonometry*. Eugene, OR: Wipf & Stock, 2003.

Websites

Agnes Scott College

www.agnesscott.edu/lriddle/women/chronol.htm

This site has a great collection of biographies of important women mathematicians down through history.

Cool Math

www.coolmath.com/precalculus-review-calculus-intro

This is a good website for a wide range of topics. Of particular note is the colorful layout for a good review of precalculus material.

Drexel University Math Forum

mathforum.org/dr.math/

This site offers a variety of basic explanations of concepts and examples. One of its strengths is that the topics are broken down by subjects and by level in school (elementary, middle, high school, college and beyond). They do a helpful job of working through example problems and also allow you to search by topic.

Get the Math

www.thirteen.org/get-the-math/

This site has some good videos geared at middle-school level that give interaction with real-life examples of mathematics in fashion, music, and other areas.

Khan Academy

www.khanacademy.org

This is an excellent online learning website, and the learn-as-you-go format allows you to click on only the short instructional videos you need as you work your way through the course. There are courses at a wide range of skill levels.

NYU Department of Mathematics—Courant Institute

cims.nyu.edu/~kiryl/precalculus.html

This is a nice, clean, visual layout of a thorough variety of topics in trigonometry and other transcendental function topics, as well as review of key ideas from algebra.

Plus Magazine

plus.maths.org/content/

This online magazine is run under the Millennium Mathematics Project at Cambridge University. It offers interesting short articles on interesting problems in math (and science). The problems are complex, but they are broken down in a way that is easy to follow.

Bibliography

Barnett, Raymond A, Michael R. Ziegler, and Karl E. Byleen. *College Algebra with Trigonometry*. New York: McGraw-Hill, 2001.

Bellos, Alex. *The Grapes of Math*. New York: Simon and Schuster, 2014.

Berlinghoff, William P., Kerry E. Grant, and Dale Skrien. *A Mathematical Sampler: Topics for Liberal Arts*. Lanham, MD: Ardsley House Publishers, 2001.

Byers, William. *How Mathematicians Think: Using Ambiguity, Contradiction, and Paradox to Create Mathematics*. Princeton, NJ: Princeton University Press, 2007.

Cady, Brendan, ed. *For All Practical Purposes: Mathematical Literacy in Today's World*. New York: W. H. Freeman and Company, 2006.

Charles, Randall I. *Algebra I: Common Core*. New York: Pearson, 2010.

Clawson, Calvin C. *Mathematical Mysteries: The Beauty and Magic of Numbers*. New York: Plenum Press, 1996.

Devlin, Keith. Mathematics: *The Science of Patterns: The Search for Order in Life, Mind and the Universe*. New York: Henry Holt, 2003.

Ellenberg, Jordan. *How Not to Be Wrong: The Power of Mathematical Thinking*. New York: Penguin, 2014.

Frenkel, Edward. *Love & Math: The Heart of Hidden Reality*. New York: Basic Books, 2013.

Gordon, John N., Ralph V. McGrew, and Raymond A. Serway. *Physics for Scientists and Engineers*. Belmont, CA: Thomson Brooks/Cole, 2005.

Jackson, Tom, editor. *Mathematics: An Illustrated History of Numbers*. New York: Shelter Harbor Press, 2012.

Lehrman, Robert L. *Physics The Easy Way*. Hauppage, NY: Barron's Educational Series, Inc., 1990.

Mankiewicz, Richard. *The Story of Mathematics*. Princeton, NJ: Princeton University Press, 2000.

McLeish, John. Numbers: *The History of Numbers and How They Shape Our Lives*. New York: Fawcett Columbine, 1991.

Oakley, Barber. *A Mind for Numbers: How to Excel at Math and Science (Even if You Flunked Algebra)*. New York: Tarcher, 2014.

Paulos, John Allen. *Beyond Numeracy: Ruminations of a Numbers Man*. New York: Alfred A. Knopf, 1991.

Peterson, Ivars. *Islands of Truth: A Mathematical Mystery Cruise*. New York: W. H. Freeman and Company, 1990.

——. *The Mathematical Tourist: Snapshots of Modern Mathematics*. New York: W. H. Freeman and Company, 1988.

Pickover, Clifford A. *The Math Book: From Pythagoras to the 57th Dimension, 250 Milestones in the History of Mathematics*. New York: Sterling, 2009.

Rooney, Anne. *The Story of Mathematics: From Creating the Pyramids to Exploring Infinity*. London: Arcturus, 2015.

Sardar, Ziauddin, Jerry Ravetz, and Borin Van Loon. *Introducing Mathematics*. Cambridge, UK: Icon Books, 1999.

Stewart, Ian. *Nature's Numbers: The Unreal Reality of Mathematics*. New York: Basic Books, 1995.

Stewart, James, Lothar Redlin, and Saleem Watson. *Elementary Functions*. Boston: Cengage Learning, 2011.

Strogatz, Steven. *The Joy of X: A Guided Tour of Math, from One to Infinity*. Boston: Houghton-Mifflin, 2012.

Index

Page numbers in **boldface** are illustrations. Entries in **boldface** are glossary terms.

About the Author

Erik Richardson is an award-winning teacher from Milwaukee, where he has taught and tutored math up to the college level over the last ten years. He has done graduate work in math, economics, and the philosophy of math, and he uses all three in his work as a business consultant with corporations and small businesses. He is a member of the Kappa Mu Epsilon math honor society, and some of his work applying math to different kinds of problems has shown up at conferences, in magazines, and even in a few pieces of published poetry. As the director of Every Einstein (everyeinstein.org), he works actively to get math and science resources into the hands of teachers and students all over the country.